Atlantic
Ocean

Pacific
Ocean

Indian
Ocean

Pacific
Ocean

HABITAT Arctic foxes live on the coast and islands of the Arctic Ocean. They live in burrows dug in the side of hills or cliffs.

CHARACTERISTICS The arctic fox uses its bushy tail to stay warm.

SELF-PROTECTION A small nose helps the arctic fox live in cold climates.

CAMOUFLAGE In the summer, the fur is short. It is brown, gray, or blue.

Science

Arctic Fox

Harcourt

SCHOOL PUBLISHERS

Orlando   Austin   New York   San Diego   Toronto   London

Visit *The Learning Site!*
www.harcourtschool.com

Arctic Fox

Consulting Authors

Michael J. Bell
*Assistant Professor of Early
Childhood Education*
College of Education
West Chester University of
Pennsylvania

Michael A. DiSpezio
Curriculum Architect
JASON Academy
Cape Cod, Massachusetts

Marjorie Frank
*Former Adjunct, Science
Education*
Hunter College
New York, New York

Gerald H. Krockover
*Professor of Earth and Atmospheric
Science Education*
Purdue University
West Lafayette, Indiana

Joyce C. McLeod
Adjunct Professor
Rollins College
Winter Park, Florida

Barbara ten Brink
Science Specialist
Austin Independent School
District
Austin, Texas

Carol J. Valenta
Senior Vice President
St. Louis Science Center
St. Louis, Missouri

Barry A. Van Deman
President and CEO
Museum of Life and Science
Durham, North Carolina

Senior Editorial Advisors

Napoleon Adebola Bryant, Jr.
Professor Emeritus of Education
Xavier University
Cincinnati, Ohio

Robert M. Jones
Professor of Educational Foundations
University of Houston-Clear Lake
Houston, Texas

Mozell P. Lang
Former Science Consultant
Michigan Department of Education
Science Consultant, Highland Park
Schools
Highland Park, Michigan

LIFE SCIENCE

EARTH SCIENCE

UNIT D: Weather, Seasons, and the Sky

Science Spin Weekly Reader

Technology Is the Weather Getting Worse?, 242

People Watching the Weather, 244

Science Spin Weekly Reader

Technology Snow Is Useful, 276

People Meet Ivy the Inventor, 278

Science Spin Weekly Reader

Technology Smart Spacesuits, 302

People Studying Mars, 304

PHYSICAL SCIENCE

Science Spin Weekly Reader

Technology
Making Driving Safer, **408**

People
Moving with Magnets, **410**

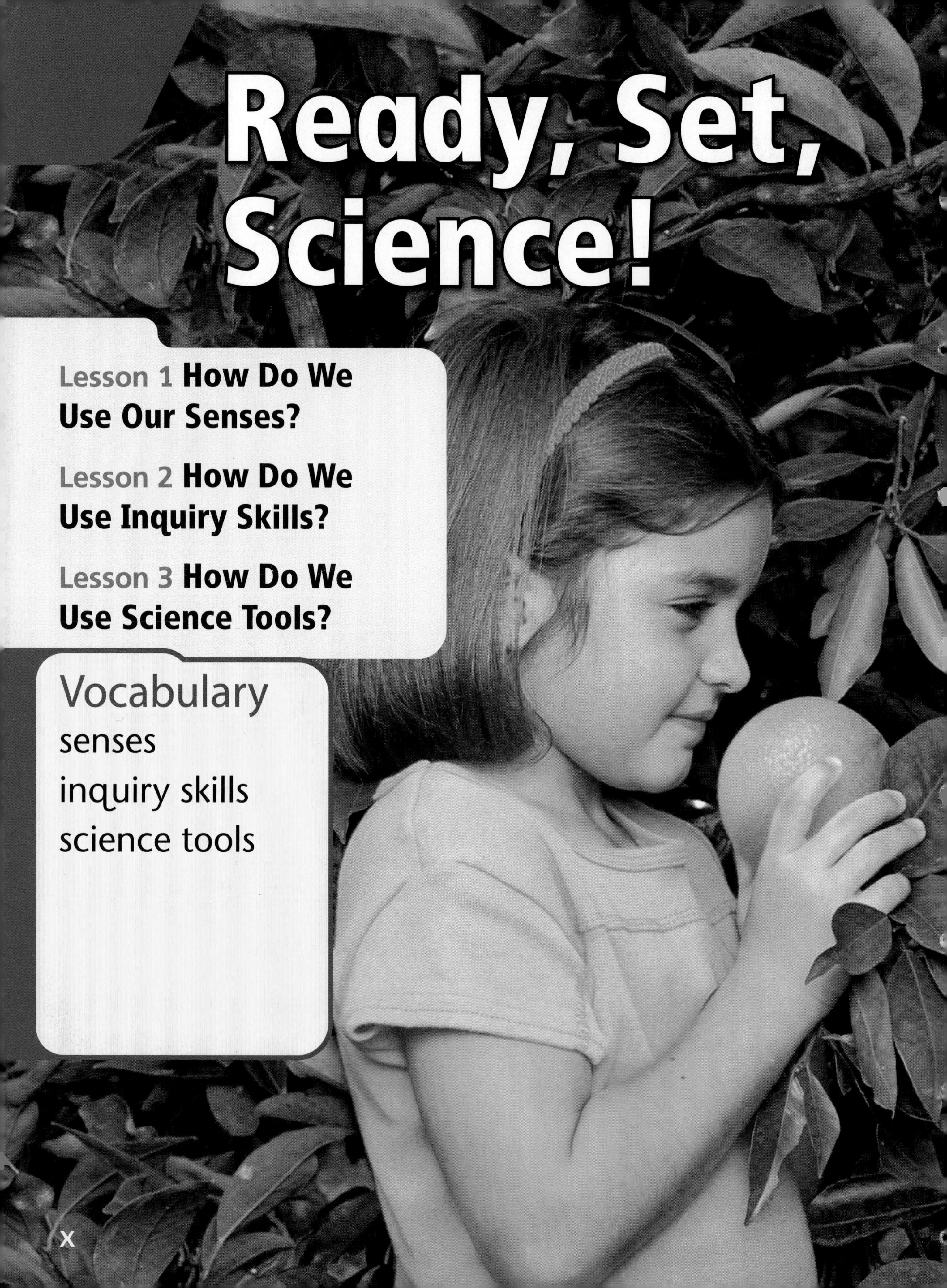

Ready, Set, Science!

Lesson 1 **How Do We Use Our Senses?**

Lesson 2 **How Do We Use Inquiry Skills?**

Lesson 3 **How Do We Use Science Tools?**

Vocabulary

senses
inquiry skills
science tools

I wonder...

Can kids be scientists?

What do **YOU** wonder?

How Do We Use Our Senses?

Fast Fact

You have about 10,000 taste buds on your tongue! You can use taste and other senses to predict things.

How Your Senses Work

You need

- oranges
- bananas
- apples

Step 1

Close your eyes. Your partner will give you a piece of fruit.

Step 2

Smell the fruit. Then taste it. **Predict** which kind of fruit you will see when you open your eyes. Was your **prediction** correct?

Step 3

Trade places with your partner. Repeat.

Inquiry Skill

When you **predict**, you tell what you think will happen.

3

VOCABULARY
senses

 READING FOCUS SKILL

MAIN IDEA AND DETAILS Look for details about using senses.

Your Senses

People have five senses. The five **senses** are sight, hearing, smell, taste, and touch. You use different body parts for different senses.

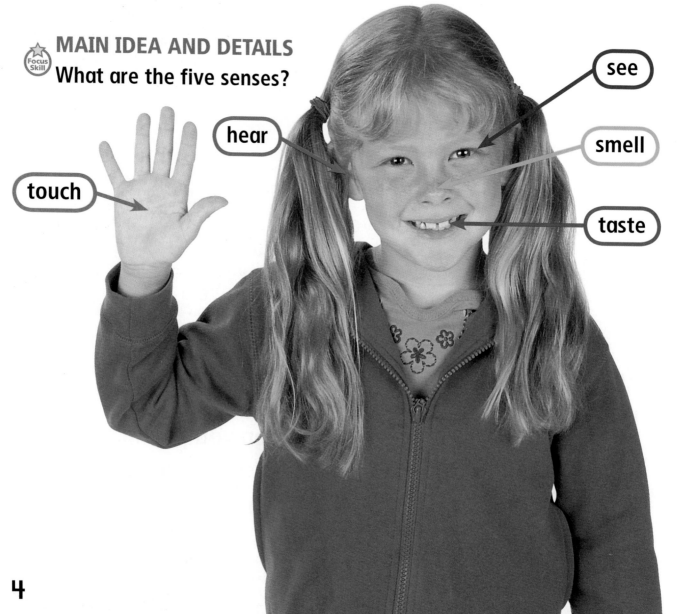

MAIN IDEA AND DETAILS
What are the five senses?

see

smell

taste

hear

touch

Senses Help You

Your senses help you observe and learn about many things.

 MAIN IDEA AND DETAILS
How can your senses help you learn?

What Do You Hear?

Close your eyes, and listen closely to the sounds around you. Predict what sounds you hear. Open your eyes. Were your predictions correct?

Using Senses Safely

Keep your body safe. Use safety equipment when you need to. Follow these safety rules.

MAIN IDEA AND DETAILS

How can you keep safe?

Wear gloves.
Wear goggles.
Wear an apron.
Don't touch anything hot.
Don't put anything in your mouth unless your teacher tells you to.

Focus Skill **1. MAIN IDEA AND DETAILS** Copy and complete this chart.

> **The Five Senses**

> **Main Idea**
> You have five senses.

| detail sight | detail Ⓐ _____ | detail Ⓑ _____ | detail Ⓒ _____ | detail touch |

2. SUMMARIZE Use the chart to tell about the lesson.

3. VOCABULARY Use the word **senses** to tell about the picture.

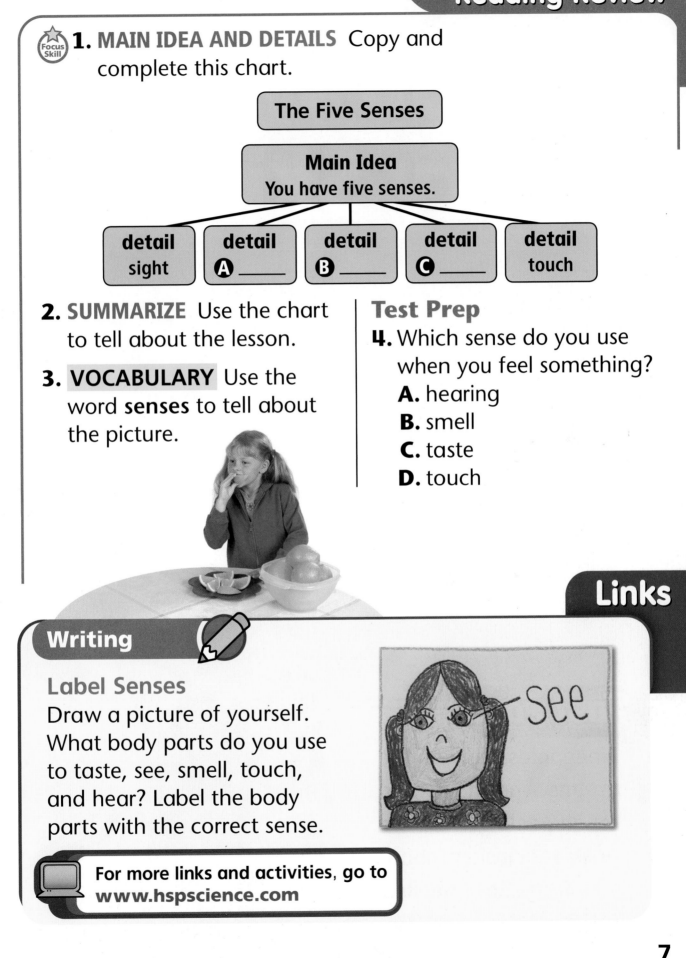

Test Prep

4. Which sense do you use when you feel something?
  A. hearing
  B. smell
  C. taste
  D. touch

Links

Writing

Label Senses
Draw a picture of yourself. What body parts do you use to taste, see, smell, touch, and hear? Label the body parts with the correct sense.

For more links and activities, go to www.hspscience.com

How Do We Use Inquiry Skills?

Fast Fact

Pineapples grow on the ground. They have hard, rough peelings. You can draw conclusions about why fruits have peelings.

Fruit Protection

You need

- **fruits**

- **hand lens**

Step 1

Observe some fruits with a hand lens. Look at their peelings.

Step 2

Observe the cut fruits with the hand lens. What is inside the fruit?

Step 3

Draw conclusions about why fruits have peelings.

Inquiry Skill

You draw conclusions when you use information to figure out why something is the way it is.

9

VOCABULARY
inquiry skills

 READING FOCUS SKILL

MAIN IDEAS AND DETAILS Look for details about the inquiry skills scientists use.

Investigating

Scientists follow steps to test things they want to learn about.

1. Observe, and ask a question.

Ask questions. What do you want to know? You can work alone, with a partner, or in a small group.

Is a balloon filled with air heavier than a balloon without air?

2. Form a hypothesis.

Explore your questions. What do you think will happen?

My Hypothesis
A balloon filled with air is heavier

3. Plan a fair test.

It is important to be fair. This will help you get correct answers to your questions.

I'll tie these at the same spot on each end.

4. Do the test.

Try your test. Repeat your test in different places. You should get the same answers.

5. Draw conclusions. Communicate what you learn.

What did you find out? Compare your answers with those of classmates. Share your answers by talking, drawing, or writing.

MAIN IDEA AND DETAILS What steps do scientists follow to test things?

11

Using Inquiry Skills

Scientists use inquiry skills when they do tests. **Inquiry skills** help people find out information.

communicate

classify

make a model

hypothesize

The red car will roll farther because it is heavier.

draw conclusions

13

compare

sequence

egg

larva

pupa

butterfly comes out

adult butterfly

measure

GO TEAM!

14

observe

predict

Life Cycle of a Bean Plant

Seed
Sprouting

Seed

Roots

plan an investigation

infer

☆ Focus Skill

MAIN IDEA AND DETAILS
What skills do scientists use when they do tests?

16

1. MAIN IDEA AND DETAILS Copy and complete this chart.

Main Idea
Inquiry skills help people find out information.

detail	detail	detail

measure   **A** _____   **B** _____

2. SUMMARIZE Use the chart to tell about the lesson.

3. VOCABULARY Use the words **inquiry skills** to tell about this picture.

Test Prep

4. What do you do when you compare?

   A. make a guess

   B. observe how things are alike and different

   C. make a plan to do something

   D. show how something works

Links

Math

Grouping Blocks

Get some blocks that are different sizes and colors. Think of ways to classify the blocks. Then classify the blocks in two different ways. Draw a picture of the ways you classified the blocks.

For more links and activities, go to www.hspscience.com

How Do We Use Science Tools?

Fast Fact

A blender is a tool that can help make many things—even medicines! You can use tools to compare things.

Compare Fruit

You need

 • strawberry • pear  • balance

Step 1

Put one piece of fruit on each side of a balance.

Step 2

Compare the masses of the fruits. Record what you see.

Step 3

Which fruit has less mass? Which has more mass?

Inquiry Skill

You **compare** when you observe ways things are alike and different.

VOCABULARY
science tools

 READING FOCUS SKILL

MAIN IDEA AND DETAILS Look for details about science tools.

Using Science Tools

Scientists use tools to find out about things. You can use tools to find out about things, too. **Science tools** help people find information they need.

Some things have parts that are too small to see. You can use a hand lens or a magnifying box to help you see them.

hand lens and magnifying box

forceps

You can use forceps to help you separate things.

dropper

You can use a dropper to place drops of liquid.

You can use a measuring cup to measure liquid.

measuring cup

thermometer

You can use a thermometer to measure how hot or cold something is.

You can use a ruler to measure how long or tall an object is. You can use a measuring tape to measure around an object.

ruler and measuring tape

balance

You can use a balance to measure the mass of an object.

Insta-Lab

Measure It!
Use a tape measure to measure around your arm. Then measure around your leg. Compare the numbers. Which one is greater?

★Focus Skill **MAIN IDEA AND DETAILS**
How can you use science tools to find out information?

22

Focus Skill

1. MAIN IDEA AND DETAILS Copy and complete this chart.

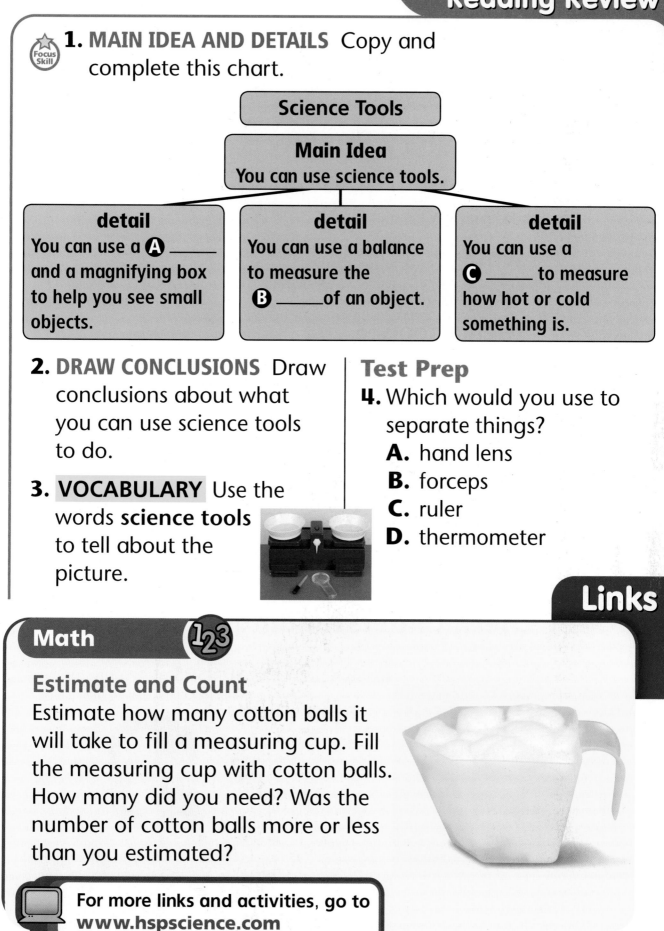

Science Tools

Main Idea
You can use science tools.

detail	detail	detail
You can use a **A** _____ and a magnifying box to help you see small objects.	You can use a balance to measure the **B** _____ of an object.	You can use a **C** _____ to measure how hot or cold something is.

2. DRAW CONCLUSIONS Draw conclusions about what you can use science tools to do.

3. VOCABULARY Use the words **science tools** to tell about the picture.

Test Prep

4. Which would you use to separate things?
  A. hand lens
  B. forceps
  C. ruler
  D. thermometer

Links

Math 1₂3

Estimate and Count
Estimate how many cotton balls it will take to fill a measuring cup. Fill the measuring cup with cotton balls. How many did you need? Was the number of cotton balls more or less than you estimated?

For more links and activities, go to www.hspscience.com

Review and Test Preparation

Vocabulary Review

Use the words to complete the sentences.

senses p. 4

inquiry skills p. 12

science tools p. 20

1. Compare and measure are two ___.

2. Smell is one of your five ___.

3. Scientists use ___ such as droppers and rulers.

Check Understanding

4. Tell **details** about the senses the girl is using in this picture.

5. When you investigate something, what is the next step after you observe and question?

    A. do the test

    B. form a hypothesis

    C. plan the test

    D. draw conclusions and communicate what you learned

Critical Thinking

6. Look at these science tools. Which would you use to make something look larger?

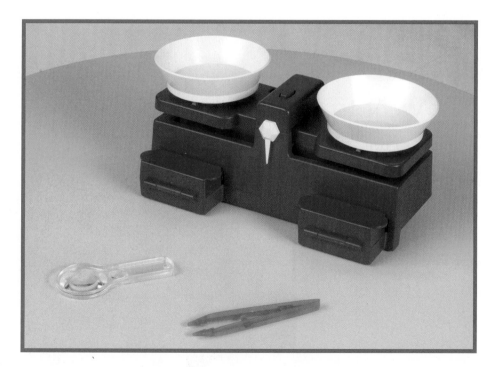

LIFE SCIENCE

Plants and Animals All Around

○○○ **St. Louis Zoo**

TO: nicholas@hspscience.com

FROM: ann@hspscience.com

RE: St. Louis Zoo

Dear Nicholas,
My class went to the zoo. I saw lots of animals. I even caught a butterfly!
Ann

TO: jimmy@hspscience.com

FROM: ashley@hspscience.com

RE: Long Island, New York

Dear Jimmy,

I saw the world's largest pumpkin!

It was heavier than a grizzly bear!

Your friend,

Ashley

Experiment!

Seeds

As you do this unit, you will find out how seeds grow. Plan and do a test. Find out if seeds need water to grow.

Chapter 1

All About Animals

Lesson 1 **What Are Living and Nonliving Things?**

Lesson 2 **What Do Animals Need?**

Lesson 3 **How Can We Group Animals?**

Lesson 4 **How Do Animals Grow and Change?**

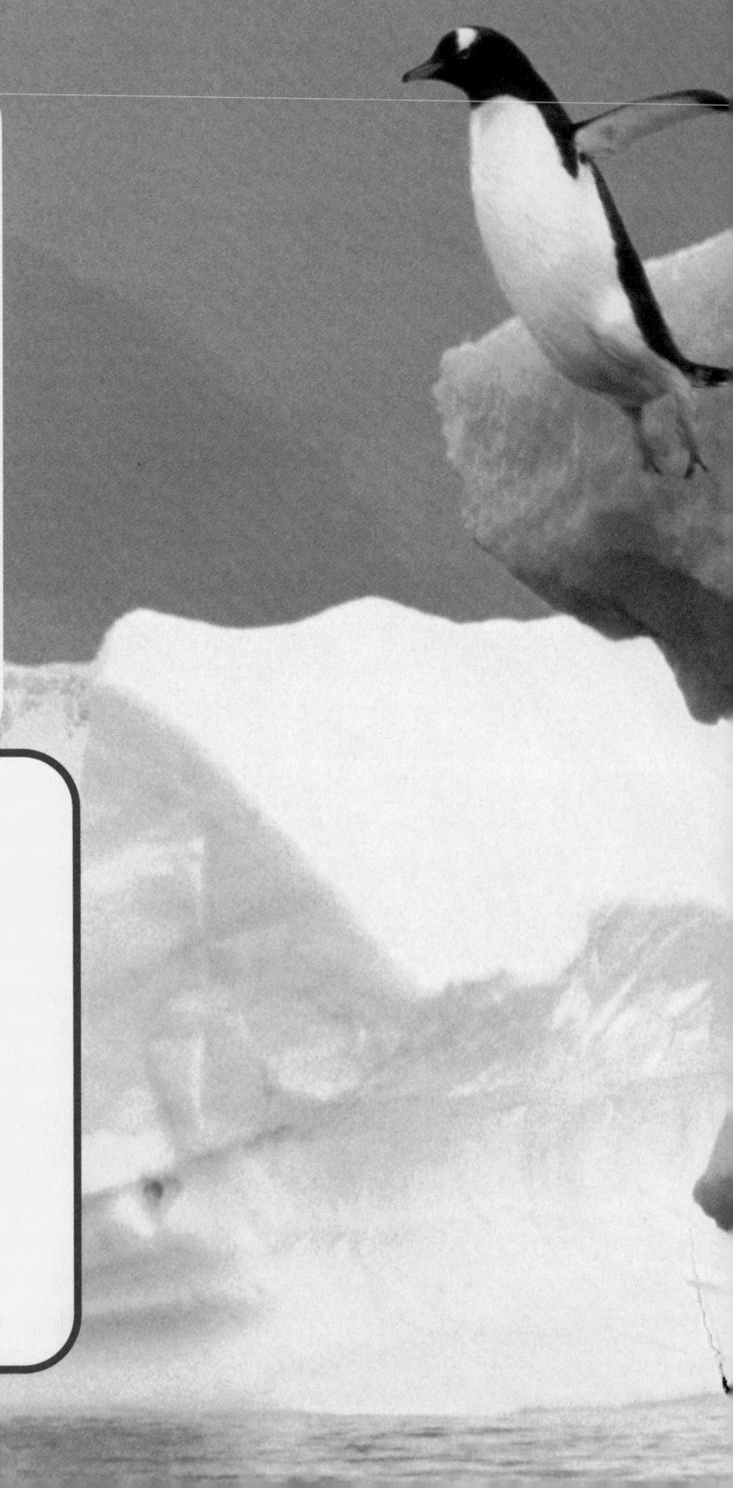

Vocabulary

living
nonliving
lungs
gills
shelter
mammal
bird
reptile
amphibian
fish
insect
life cycle
tadpole
larva
pupa

I wonder...

How do penguins stay warm?

What do you wonder?

What Are Living and Nonliving Things?

Living and Nonliving Things

You need

 • mealworm   • rock   • bran meal and box   • hand lens

Step 1

Put the mealworm, rock, and bran meal in a box. Observe with the hand lens.

Step 2

Does the mealworm eat or move? Does the rock eat or move? Draw what you see.

Step 3

Classify the mealworm and the rock as living things or nonliving things.

Inquiry Skill

When you classify things, you can see how they are alike and different.

31

VOCABULARY

living
nonliving

 **READING FOCUS SKILL**

COMPARE AND CONTRAST Look for ways living things and nonliving things are alike and different.

Living and Nonliving Things

Living things need food, water, and air. They all grow and change. Plants and animals are living things.

> Which things in this picture are living? Which are nonliving?

wolf

rocks

Nonliving things do not need food, water, or air. They do not grow. Rocks and water are nonliving things.

 COMPARE AND CONTRAST How are all nonliving things alike?

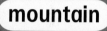 mountain

 plants

water

 Insta-Lab

Compare Living Things
Look at a living thing. Draw what you see. Then compare your picture with a partner's picture. Are both things living? Talk about how you know.

Classify Living and Nonliving Things

You can classify things as living or nonliving. Living things need food, water, and air. They grow and change. If something is not like living things in these two ways, then it is nonliving.

Living	Nonliving

 COMPARE AND CONTRAST Look at the chart. How are the living things different from the nonliving things?

Focus Skill

1. COMPARE AND CONTRAST Copy and complete this chart.

Living Things	Nonliving Things
They need **A** _____.	They do not need food.
They need water.	They do not need **B** _____.
They need **C** _____.	They do not need **D** _____.
They grow and **E** _____.	They do not **F** _____ and change.

2. SUMMARIZE Use the chart to write a lesson summary.

3. VOCABULARY Use the words **living** and **nonliving** to talk about the picture.

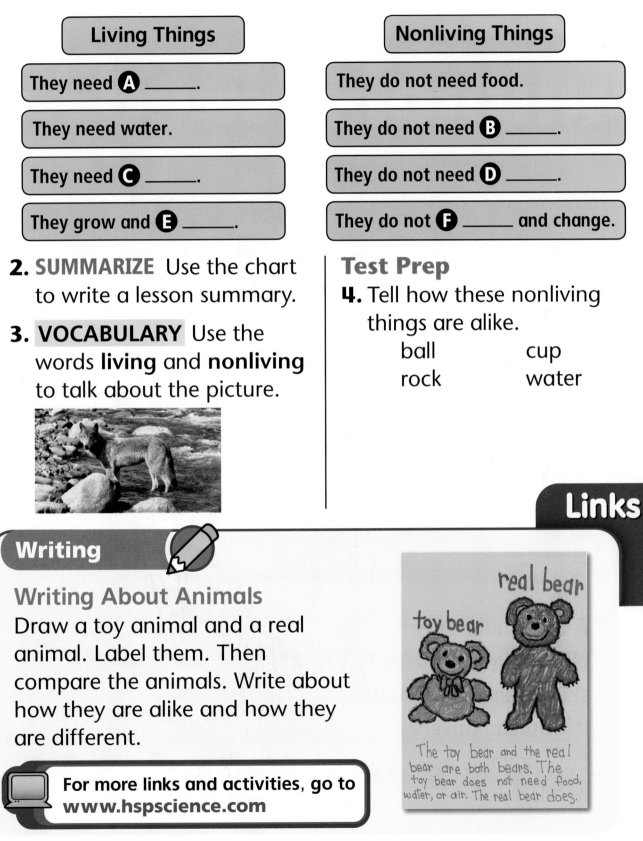

Test Prep

4. Tell how these nonliving things are alike.

ball   cup
rock   water

Links

Writing

Writing About Animals
Draw a toy animal and a real animal. Label them. Then compare the animals. Write about how they are alike and how they are different.

For more links and activities, go to www.hspscience.com

real bear

toy bear

The toy bear and the real bear are both bears. The toy bear does not need food, water, or air. The real bear does.

35

What Do Animals Need?

Fast Fact

A caterpillar eats almost all the time. It sheds its skin when it outgrows it. You can observe how animals meet their needs.

Observe an Animal Home

You need

- plastic box and gloves
- soil, twig, leaf, rocks
- water in a bottle cap
- small animals

Step 1

Put the soil, twig, leaf, rocks, and water in the box. Add the animals.

Step 2

Observe. Draw what you see.

Step 3

Tell how the home you made gives the animals food, water, and a place to live.

Inquiry Skill

Observe the animals in their home to see how they meet their needs.

37

VOCABULARY

lungs
gills
shelter

 READING FOCUS SKILL

MAIN IDEA AND DETAILS Look for the four things all animals need to live.

Animals Need Food and Water

Animals need food to live and grow. Pandas eat bamboo.

Animals need water, too. Zebras and giraffes drink from ponds. They also get water from foods they eat.

 MAIN IDEA AND DETAILS What are two things animals need to live?

panda

giraffe

zebra

Animals Need Air

All animals need air. They have body parts that help them breathe. Giraffes and zebras have lungs. **Lungs** help some animals breathe air. Fish have gills. **Gills** take air from water.

 MAIN IDEA AND DETAILS
What are two body parts animals use to get air?

Pet Food Survey

Take a survey. List some pet foods. Then ask classmates what their pets eat. Put a tally mark next to each food. Which food is eaten by most children's pets?

Animals Need Shelter

Most animals need shelter. A **shelter** is a place where an animal can be safe. Some birds use a tree as shelter. A hole in the ground is a shelter for foxes.

 MAIN IDEA AND DETAILS
Why does a bird use a tree as shelter?

owl

foxes

Focus Skill **1. MAIN IDEA AND DETAILS** Copy and complete this chart.

Animal Needs

- **food**
  - Animals need food to live.
- **water**
  - Some get water by drinking.
  - Some get it from the **A** _____ they eat.
- **air**
  - Some get air with **B** _____.
  - Some get it with gills.
- **shelter**
  - Shelter is a place to be **C** _____.

2. DRAW CONCLUSIONS What are four things that animals need?

3. VOCABULARY Use the word **shelter** to talk about this picture.

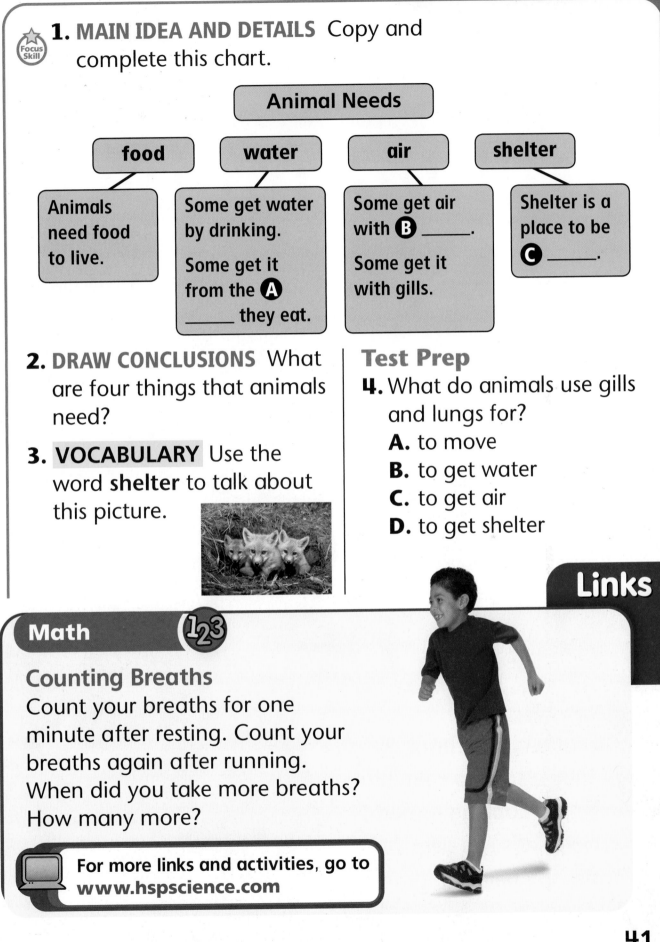

Test Prep

4. What do animals use gills and lungs for?
- **A.** to move
- **B.** to get water
- **C.** to get air
- **D.** to get shelter

Links

Math 123

Counting Breaths
Count your breaths for one minute after resting. Count your breaths again after running. When did you take more breaths? How many more?

For more links and activities, go to **www.hspscience.com**

How Can We Group Animals?

Fast Fact

Feathers help birds fly. They also help keep birds warm. Looking at body coverings can help you classify animals.

Classify Animals

You need

- crayons

- paper

Step 1

Observe different kinds of animals.

Step 2

Draw pictures to record your observations.

Step 3

Classify the animals into groups. Tell how you **classified** the animals in each group.

Inquiry Skill

Classify animals to help you see how they are alike and different.

READING FOCUS SKILL

MAIN IDEA AND DETAILS Look for the main idea and details about each kind of animal.

Mammals

A **mammal** is an animal that has hair or fur. Almost all mammals give birth to live young. The young drink milk from their mother's body.

 MAIN IDEA AND DETAILS
What is a mammal?

seal and pup

tiger

bird feeding chicks

Birds

A **bird** is the only kind of animal that has feathers. Most birds use their wings to fly. Birds have their young by laying eggs. They find food to feed their young.

⭐ **MAIN IDEA AND DETAILS**

Focus Skill

How can you tell if an animal is a bird?

peacock

Reptiles and Amphibians

A **reptile** has scaly, dry skin. Lizards and turtles are reptiles.

turtle

gecko

Most **amphibians** have smooth, wet skin. Young amphibians hatch from eggs that are laid in the water. As adults, they live on land. Frogs are amphibians.

frog

MAIN IDEA AND DETAILS
What kind of animal has smooth, wet skin?

red soldier fish

Fish

Most **fish** are covered with scales. Fish live in water. They use gills to breathe.

 MAIN IDEA AND DETAILS
How do fish breathe?

sailfish

Insects

An **insect** is an animal that
has three body parts and six legs.
Insects do not have bones. A hard
shell keeps their soft insides safe.

⭐ **Focus Skill** **MAIN IDEA AND DETAILS** How many
parts does an insect's body have?

beetle

ants

Insta-Lab

How Many Legs?
Count the legs of
animals in this lesson.
Use the data to make
a chart. Then use your
chart to compare
numbers of legs.

butterfly

Focus Skill

1. MAIN IDEA AND DETAILS Copy and complete this chart.

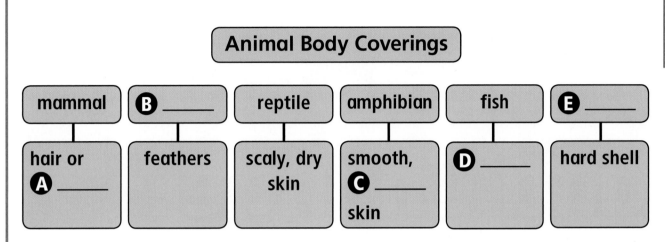

Animal Body Coverings

mammal	B _____	reptile	amphibian	fish	E _____
hair or A _____	feathers	scaly, dry skin	smooth, C _____ skin	D _____	hard shell

2. DRAW CONCLUSIONS
Which two animal groups do you think are the most alike? Explain.

3. VOCABULARY
Use the word **bird** to tell about this animal.

Test Prep

4. What kind of animal feeds its young with milk from its body?
  A. a bird
  B. a fish
  C. an insect
  D. a mammal

Links

Art

Patterned Wrapping Paper
Make animal-pattern wrapping paper. Look at patterns on butterfly wings and on other animals. Choose a pattern you like. Copy it onto a large piece of paper. Color it with crayons or paint.

For more links and activities, go to
www.hspscience.com

Lesson **4**

How Do Animals Grow and Change?

Fast Fact

A newborn polar bear weighs less than this book. An adult weighs as much as a car! Compare to see how animals grow and change.

50

Animals Grow and Change

You need

- **animal picture cards**

Step 1

Look at the picture cards. Match each adult animal with its young.

Step 2

Make a chart to **compare** adult animals with their young.

Animals and Their Young

Animal	Same	Different
sea turtles	Both have flippers.	One is big. One is small.

Step 3

Write about how each adult animal is like its young and how it is different.

Inquiry Skill

Compare adult animals and their young. How are they alike and different?

51

Reading in Science

VOCABULARY

life cycle
tadpole
larva
pupa

 READING FOCUS SKILL

SEQUENCE Look for ways each animal changes as it grows.

How a Frog Grows

A **life cycle** is all of the parts of an animal's life.

A frog's life cycle starts as an egg in water. A **tadpole**, or young frog, comes out of the egg. Its tail helps it swim. It breathes with gills.

eggs

about 7 weeks

about 2 weeks

The tadpole grows legs, and its tail gets smaller. It starts to use lungs to breathe. Soon it is an adult frog. It lives on land most of the time.

⭐ Focus Skill **SEQUENCE** How does a tadpole change as it grows?

about 14 weeks

about 9 weeks

How a Butterfly Grows

A butterfly also starts its life cycle as an egg. A **larva**, or caterpillar, comes out of the egg. The larva eats and grows.

The larva stops eating. It becomes a **pupa** with a hard covering. Inside, the pupa changes into a butterfly. At last, an adult butterfly comes out.

SEQUENCE What happens after the larva stops eating?

egg

larva

adult butterfly

butterfly comes out

pupa

Insta-Lab

Be a Butterfly

Act out a butterfly's life cycle. What happens first, next, and last? How can you move your body to show what happens?

Animals and Their Young

Dogs are mammals. The puppies look like their parents, but they are not just like them. They are not just like each other. Each puppy is a little different.

How does a puppy change as it grows?

How is it like its parents?

just-born puppies

about 2 months old

adult dog

For more links and activities, go to www.hspscience.com

Focus Skill **1. SEQUENCE** Copy and complete this chart.

Life Cycle of A Butterfly

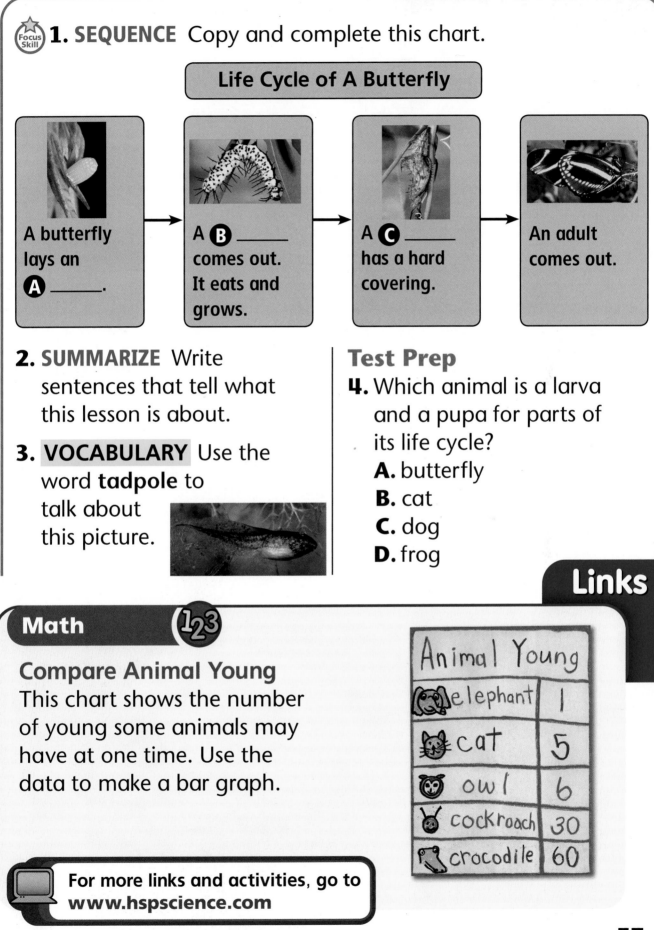

A butterfly lays an **A** ____.

A **B** ____ comes out. It eats and grows.

A **C** ____ has a hard covering.

An adult comes out.

2. SUMMARIZE Write sentences that tell what this lesson is about.

3. VOCABULARY Use the word **tadpole** to talk about this picture.

Test Prep

4. Which animal is a larva and a pupa for parts of its life cycle?

A. butterfly
B. cat
C. dog
D. frog

Links

Math 123

Compare Animal Young
This chart shows the number of young some animals may have at one time. Use the data to make a bar graph.

Animal Young	
elephant	1
cat	5
owl	6
cockroach	30
crocodile	60

For more links and activities, go to www.hspscience.com

Traveling Turtles:

A Trip Across the Atlantic

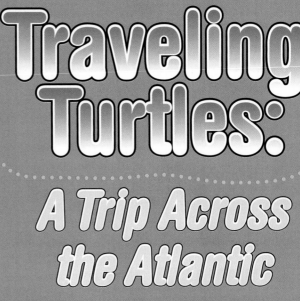

In late spring, huge sea turtles crawl onto a beach in Florida. Each turtle digs a nest in the sand. The mother turtle then lays about 100 eggs. Two months later, tiny turtles hatch.

The young turtles crawl out of their holes and into the ocean.

A Long Trip

The tiny turtles set out on a long trip. They swim across the Atlantic Ocean and back again. The trip takes between five and ten years. The trip is thousands of miles long.

Scientists wanted to know how the turtles made their way across the ocean. To find out, scientists put "bathing suits" on some young sea turtles. The bathing suits were tied to special machines. The special machines can follow how the turtles swim.

THINK ABOUT IT

How long will it take for a young turtle to swim across the Atlantic Ocean?

Find out more! Log on to
www.hspscience.com

59

Feeding Time

Chloe Ruiz went to the petting zoo with her family. Chloe saw pigs, horses, and cows.

The people at the zoo asked Chloe if she wanted to help feed a young cow. A young cow is called a calf.

Chloe fed the calf milk. She used a bottle to feed the calf. She knows the calf needs to drink lots of milk to help it grow.

Which Foods Birds Eat

What to Do

1. Put bread crumbs in one pie plate. Put fruit in the other.
2. Put both plates on a table outside.
3. Observe the birds that eat from each plate. Draw pictures to record your observations.

Materials
- 2 foil pie plates
- bread crumbs
- chopped apples and grapes

Draw Conclusions
Do different birds eat different foods? How do you know?

Animals and Their Young

Mammals and most birds care for their young. Choose one. Find out how it helps its young. Make models to show how the animal cares for its young.

Review and Test Preparation

Vocabulary Review

Tell which picture goes best with each word.

1. **mammal** p. 44
2. **bird** p. 45
3. **fish** p. 47
4. **insect** p. 48

A.  B.  C.  D.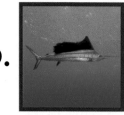

Check Understanding

5. Show the **sequence**. Write **first**, **next**, **then**, and **last**.

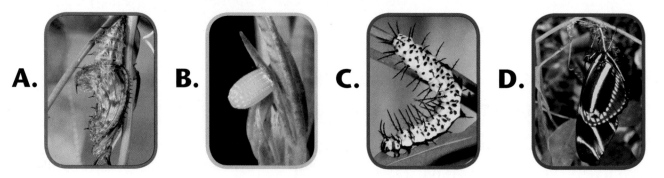

A.   B.   C.   D.

6. Which is **true** about frogs?

   A. They are fish.

   B. They have scaly, dry skin.

   C. The young are called tadpoles.

   D. Adults breathe with gills.

Critical Thinking

7. Compare the pigs. Which one is
 living? Which is not? Tell how you
know.

8. Think about a pet you want. Draw
a picture of the pet. List each thing
it needs. Tell how you would help it
meet its needs.

2 All About Plants

Vocabulary

sunlight	fruits
nutrients	seeds
roots	seed coat
stem	edible
leaves	nonedible
flowers	

I wonder...

Why do plants need water?

What do you wonder?

What Do Plants Need?

Predict What Plants Need

You need

- index cards
- 2 small plants
- spray bottle

Step 1

Label the plants. Put both plants in a sunny place.

Step 2

Water only one plant each day. **Predict** what will happen to each plant.

Step 3

After four days, check the plants. Did you **predict** correctly?

Inquiry Skill

To **predict** use what you know to make a good guess about what will happen.

67

READING FOCUS SKILL

CAUSE AND EFFECT Look for all the things that cause plants to grow.

Light, Air, and Water

A plant needs light, air, and water to make its own food. The food helps the plant grow and stay healthy. A plant also needs water to move the food to all its parts.

sunlight

air

water

Plants take in **sunlight**, or light from the sun. They take in water mostly from the soil.

⭐ **CAUSE AND EFFECT**
What would happen to a plant that did not have light, air, or water?

Insta-Lab

Make a Model Plant
Use paper, clay, craft sticks, and other art materials to make a model plant. Then tell about what a real plant needs to live.

Soil

Plants take in nutrients from the soil. **Nutrients** are minerals that plants use to make their food.

CAUSE AND EFFECT Why does a plant need nutrients?

soil

Focus Skill

1. CAUSE AND EFFECT Copy and complete this chart.

Needs of Plants

cause

A plant gets light, **A** _____, **B** _____, and nutrients.

effect

The plant grows and stays **C** _____.

2. DRAW CONCLUSIONS
What would happen if a plant did not get all the things it needed? Tell why.

3. VOCABULARY Use the words **sunlight** and **nutrients** to tell about this picture.

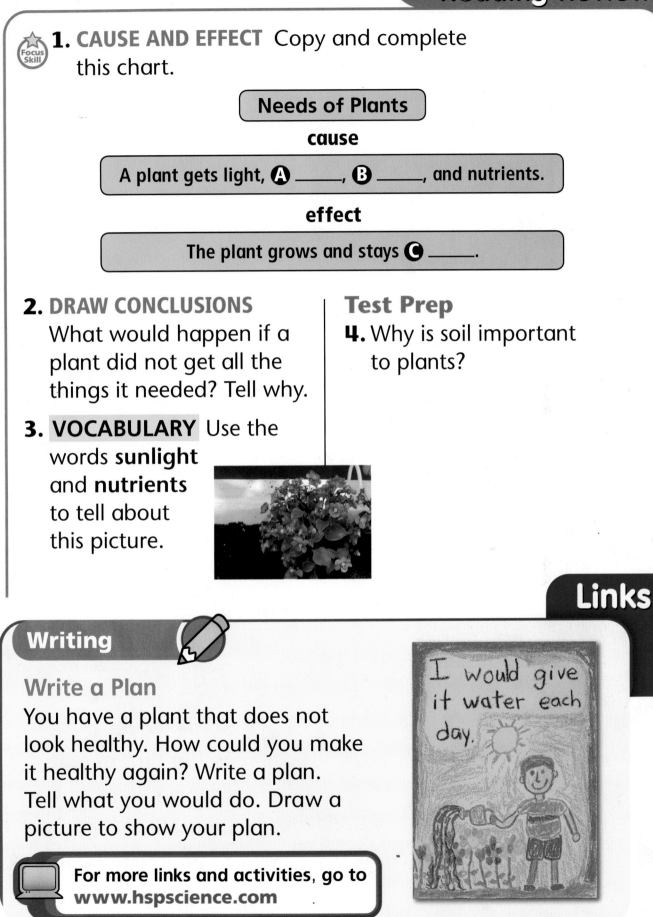

Test Prep

4. Why is soil important to plants?

Links

Writing

Write a Plan
You have a plant that does not look healthy. How could you make it healthy again? Write a plan. Tell what you would do. Draw a picture to show your plan.

I would give it water each day.

For more links and activities, go to
www.hspscience.com

What Are the Parts of a Plant?

Fast Fact

Some leaves are so big that people can use them as umbrellas! You can communicate about the parts of a plant.

Parts of a Plant

You need

• **hand lens**

• **plant**

Observe the parts of the plant. Use a hand lens.

Draw what you see.
Write about your picture.

Share your work with a partner. **Communicate** what you observed.

Inquiry Skill

You can use drawing, writing, and talking to **communicate** what you observe.

Focus Skill **READING FOCUS SKILL**

MAIN IDEA AND DETAILS Look for the parts of a plant and details about what the parts do.

Parts of a Plant

Plants have different parts. The parts help the plant live and grow. Most kinds of plants have roots, a stem, leaves, and flowers.

Focus Skill **MAIN IDEA AND DETAILS**
What are some parts of a plant?

flower

stem

leaf

roots

Roots

The **roots** hold the plant in the soil. They also take in the water and nutrients the plant needs.

 MAIN IDEA AND DETAILS
What are two ways roots help a plant?

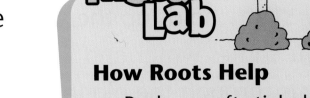

Insta-Lab

How Roots Help

Push a craft stick deep into clay. Push another craft stick into clay just a little. Tap the side of each stick. What happens? How is the first stick like a plant with roots? How do roots hold a plant in place?

Where are the roots on these plants?

75

Stems

The **stem** holds up the plant. It carries water and nutrients through the plant.

Stems may be green or woody. The trunks of trees are woody stems.

⭐ **MAIN IDEA AND DETAILS**

What are two ways the stem helps a plant?

Where are the stems on these plants?

Leaves

Leaves take in light and air. They need these things to make food for the plant. Different kinds of plants have leaves that look different. Leaves have different patterns.

 MAIN IDEA AND DETAILS
What do leaves do?

What shapes and patterns do these leaves have?

Flowers, Fruits, and Seeds

Many plants have flowers. The **flowers** make fruits. The **fruits** hold seeds.

New plants may grow from the **seeds**. The new plants look like the plants that made the seeds.

⭐ *Focus Skill*
MAIN IDEA AND DETAILS
What do flowers do?

seeds

flower

fruit

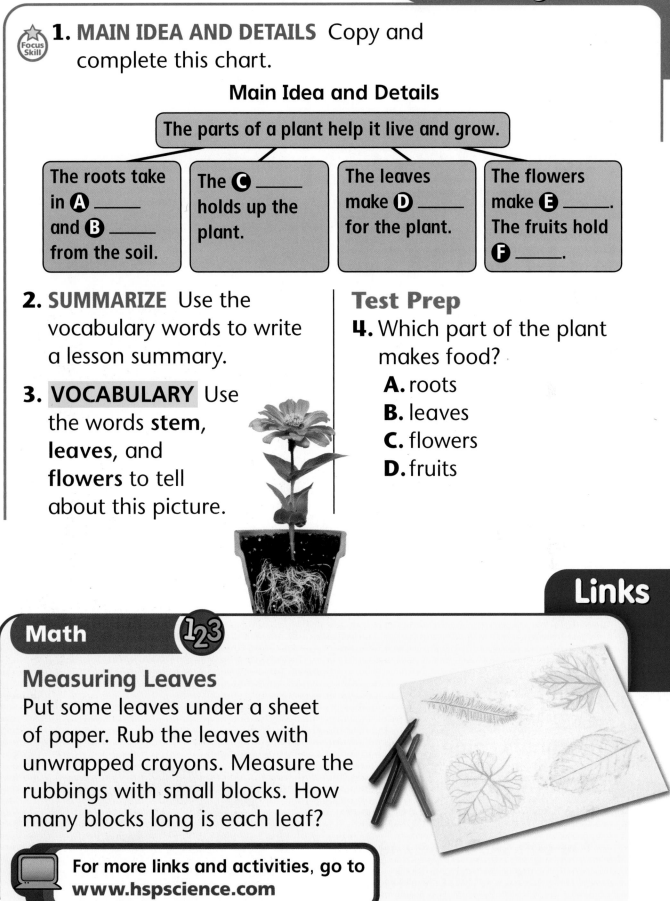

Focus Skill

1. MAIN IDEA AND DETAILS Copy and complete this chart.

Main Idea and Details

The parts of a plant help it live and grow.

The roots take in **A** _____ and **B** _____ from the soil.	The **C** _____ holds up the plant.	The leaves make **D** _____ for the plant.	The flowers make **E** _____. The fruits hold **F** _____.

2. SUMMARIZE Use the vocabulary words to write a lesson summary.

3. VOCABULARY Use the words **stem**, **leaves**, and **flowers** to tell about this picture.

Test Prep

4. Which part of the plant makes food?

A. roots
B. leaves
C. flowers
D. fruits

Links

Math

Measuring Leaves
Put some leaves under a sheet of paper. Rub the leaves with unwrapped crayons. Measure the rubbings with small blocks. How many blocks long is each leaf?

For more links and activities, go to www.hspscience.com

How Do Plants Grow and Change?

Fast Fact

Coconuts come from coconut palms. They are the world's biggest seeds. You can sequence the parts of a plant's life.

From Seed to Plant

You need

- seeds
- 2 clear cups
- colored cup
- soil

Step 1

Fill one clear cup with soil. Plant two seeds near the side. Water the seeds.

Step 2

Put the clear cup into the colored cup. Take it out each day, draw the seeds, and put it back.

Step 3

After three days, sequence your pictures to show what happened to the seeds.

Inquiry Skill

When you sequence things, you say what happened first, next, then, and last.

VOCABULARY

seed coat

(Focus Skill) **READING FOCUS SKILL**

SEQUENCE Look for what happens first, next, then, and last as a seed grows into a plant.

How Plants Grow

Most plants grow from seeds. Some seeds have a seed coat. A **seed coat** is a covering that protects the seed. Inside the seed is a tiny plant. If the seed gets water, air, and warmth, the plant in it may start to grow.

seed

seed coat

15 days

First, the roots grow down into the soil. Next, a stem grows up. Then, leaves and flowers grow. Last, the flowers make fruits that hold seeds. The seeds may grow into new plants.

⭐ **SEQUENCE** **What happens after the flowers grow?**

60 days

45 days

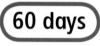

What's Inside?

Peel the seed coat off a bean seed. Then open the seed. Use a hand lens to observe what is inside. Can you find the tiny plant?

83

How Pine Trees Grow

Like other plants, most trees grow from seeds. Roots grow down. A green stem grows up. As it grows, the stem becomes woody. The stem of a tree is called a trunk.

When this tree is an adult, it makes cones. The cones hold seeds for new trees. Year after year, more branches and new cones grow. The trunk grows taller and thicker.

SEQUENCE **What happens to a tree year after year?**

cones

seed sprouting

seedling

adult tree

small tree

Seeds

Seeds may look different, but they are the same in an important way. They can grow into new plants. The new plant will look like the plant that made the seed.

Where are the seeds in these pictures?

peas

strawberry

sunflower

avocado

pepper

For more links and activities, go to www.hspscience.com

1. SEQUENCE Copy and complete this chart.

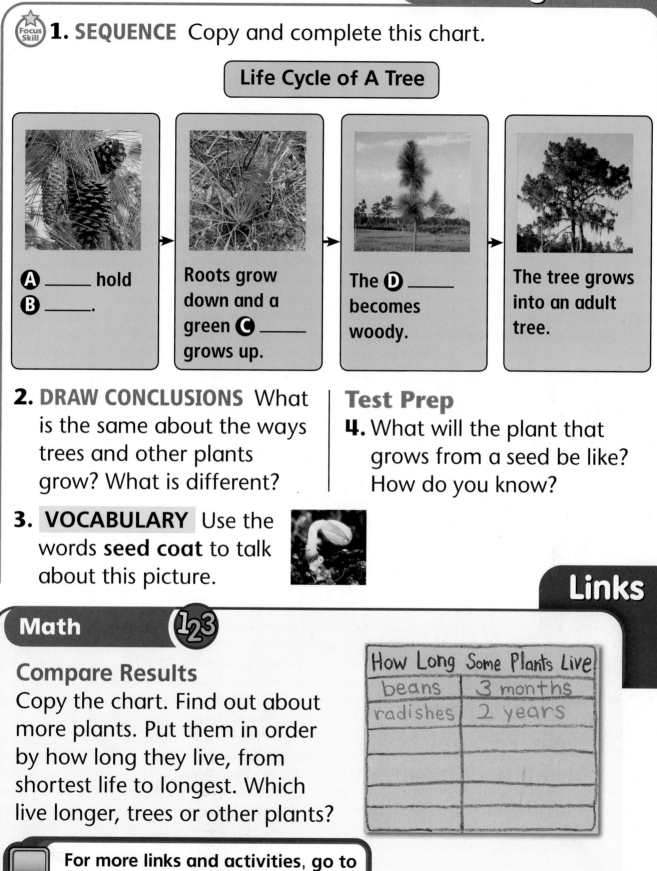

Life Cycle of A Tree

A _____ hold
B _____.

→ Roots grow down and a green **C** _____ grows up.

→ The **D** _____ becomes woody.

→ The tree grows into an adult tree.

2. DRAW CONCLUSIONS What is the same about the ways trees and other plants grow? What is different?

3. VOCABULARY Use the words **seed coat** to talk about this picture.

Test Prep

4. What will the plant that grows from a seed be like? How do you know?

Links

Math

Compare Results
Copy the chart. Find out about more plants. Put them in order by how long they live, from shortest life to longest. Which live longer, trees or other plants?

How Long Some Plants Live	
beans	3 months
radishes	2 years

For more links and activities, go to **www.hspscience.com**

87

How Can We Group Plants?

Fast Fact

There are many kinds of trees. Each tree has leaves that look different. You can classify plants by ways they are alike and different.

Classify Leaves

You need

- **6 leaves**

- **index cards**

Compare the leaves.
Do you see any patterns?
Classify them into
two groups.

Use index cards to make
labels for the groups.

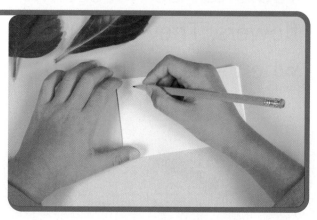

Tell how you classified
your leaves.

Inquiry Skill

When you **classify**, you
put things into groups by
ways they are alike.

VOCABULARY
edible
nonedible

 READING FOCUS SKILL

COMPARE AND CONTRAST Look for ways plants are alike and different.

Grouping Plants

One way to group plants is by looking at their parts. Grasses are one kind of plant. They all have long, thin leaves. They also have very small flowers. You often do not see the flowers. They get cut off when you cut the grass.

grass

grass

90

Trees and shrubs are groups of plants. They both have woody stems. Most trees have one big main stem. Shrubs have many smaller stems. Some trees and shrubs may have flowers, too.

⭐ **COMPARE AND CONTRAST**
How are these plants alike and different?

tree

shrub

91

Plants You Can Eat

You can group plants by whether it is safe to eat them. **Edible** things are safe to eat. Some kinds of plants that have edible parts are tomatoes, onions, and squash.

What edible plants can you get at this market?

Plants you can not eat safely are **nonedible** plants. These flowers are nonedible plants.

⭐ Focus Skill
COMPARE AND CONTRAST
What is the difference between edible plants and nonedible plants?

Looking at Lunch

Observe your lunch. Draw a picture of it. Label the parts that come from plants. What are some kinds of plants you eat?

Ways We Use Plants

You can make groups of plants that people use to make things. People use cotton to make clothing and trees to make houses and toys.

⭐ Focus Skill **COMPARE AND CONTRAST**
How are cotton plants and trees alike?

cotton

cotton shirt

wooden toy

pine tree

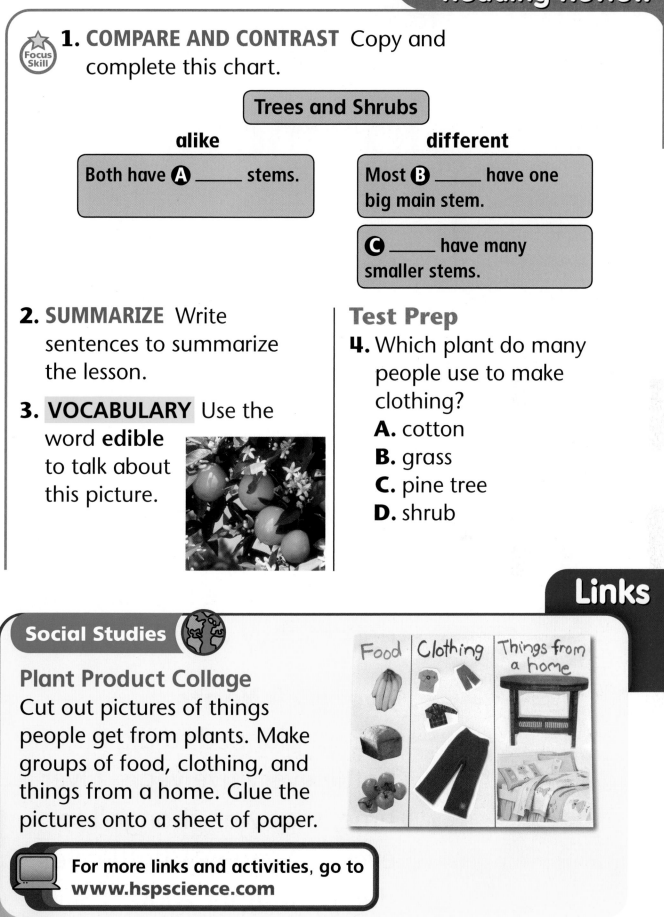

Focus Skill

1. COMPARE AND CONTRAST Copy and complete this chart.

Trees and Shrubs

alike

Both have **A** _____ stems.

different

Most **B** _____ have one big main stem.

C _____ have many smaller stems.

2. SUMMARIZE Write sentences to summarize the lesson.

3. VOCABULARY Use the word **edible** to talk about this picture.

Test Prep

4. Which plant do many people use to make clothing?
   A. cotton
   B. grass
   C. pine tree
   D. shrub

Links

Social Studies

Plant Product Collage
Cut out pictures of things people get from plants. Make groups of food, clothing, and things from a home. Glue the pictures onto a sheet of paper.

Food   Clothing   Things from a home

For more links and activities, go to www.hspscience.com

Late Bloomers

William Beal was a scientist. He lived about 125 years ago in Michigan. He put sand and seeds in 20 bottles. Then he buried the bottles in the ground.

Beal wanted to see if the seeds could still grow after being buried for a long time. The seeds were kept dry and dark so they would not grow.

Every 20 Years

Beal planned to dig up one bottle every five years. Over time, that was changed to every 20 years. A bottle was dug up in April 2000.

People dug up the bottle and planted the seeds. 26 of the 1,000 seeds grew into bright yellow flowers.

Important Work

The study helps people learn about soil and plants. It shows why weeds can grow in a plowed field. The work also helps scientists learn how seeds can live through fires and floods.

THINK ABOUT IT

Why was it important to keep the seeds in a dry, dark place?

Find out more! Log on to
www.hspscience.com

THE Plant DOCTOR

George Washington Carver was a plant scientist. Some people called him "the plant doctor." Carver worked with farmers who grew crops. He showed them how to plant peanuts to keep their soil healthy.

Carver thought of 300 things to make with peanut plants! Can you imagine washing your hair with shampoo made from peanuts? He also made foods, medicines, soaps, paints, rubber, gasoline and paper—all from the peanut plant.

98

Investigate Different Plants' Needs

Materials
- 3 different kinds of plants

What to Do

1. Do all plants need exactly the same things? Get three plants. Plan an investigation to answer the question.

2. Follow your plan.

3. Draw pictures and write sentences to record what happens.

Draw Conclusions
Did you answer the question? If not, how could you change your investigation?

How Seeds Get Around

Wind, water, and animals move seeds from place to place. Get different seeds or pictures of seeds. Observe each seed. Then find out what kind of seed it is and how it is moved. Use books and other resources.

Review and Test Preparation

Vocabulary Review

Look at the numbers next to the plant parts. Tell the number and the name of each part.

roots p. 75   **flowers** p. 78

stem p. 76   **fruit** p. 78

leaves p. 77   **seeds** p. 78

5.

1.

2.

3.

4.

6.

Check Understanding

7. What happens to a plant that gets air, light, water, and nutrients? Tell how you know.

8. You can eat corn. Which group does it belong in?

   A. edible plants   **C.** water

   B. nonedible plants   **D.** trees

Critical Thinking

Over time, Hayden observes this tree in her back yard.

9. What is happening in each picture?

10. Predict what will happen to this tree next year. Tell how you know.

Living Together

LIFE SCIENCE

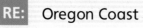
Sea Lion Caves

TO: jasmine@hspscience.com

FROM: corey@hspscience.com

RE: Oregon Coast

Dear Jasmine,
I saw the biggest
sea cave in the
world! It is the
home of sea lions.
Your pen pal,
Corey

TO: vanessa@hspscience.com

FROM: jose@hspscience.com

RE: East Lansing, Michigan

Dear Vanessa,

I went to a garden filled with flowers. The colors of the flowers were just like the colors of our crayons. It was cool!

Jose

Experiment!

Animal Coverings

As you do this unit, you will see where plants and animals live. Plan and do a test. See how animal coverings help them live where they do.

Chapter 3

Environments for Living Things

Lesson 1 **What Is an Environment?**

Lesson 2 **What Helps Plants and Animals Live in Places?**

Lesson 3 **How Do Plants and Animals Need Each Other?**

Vocabulary

environment
adaptation
camouflage
oxygen
pollen
food chain

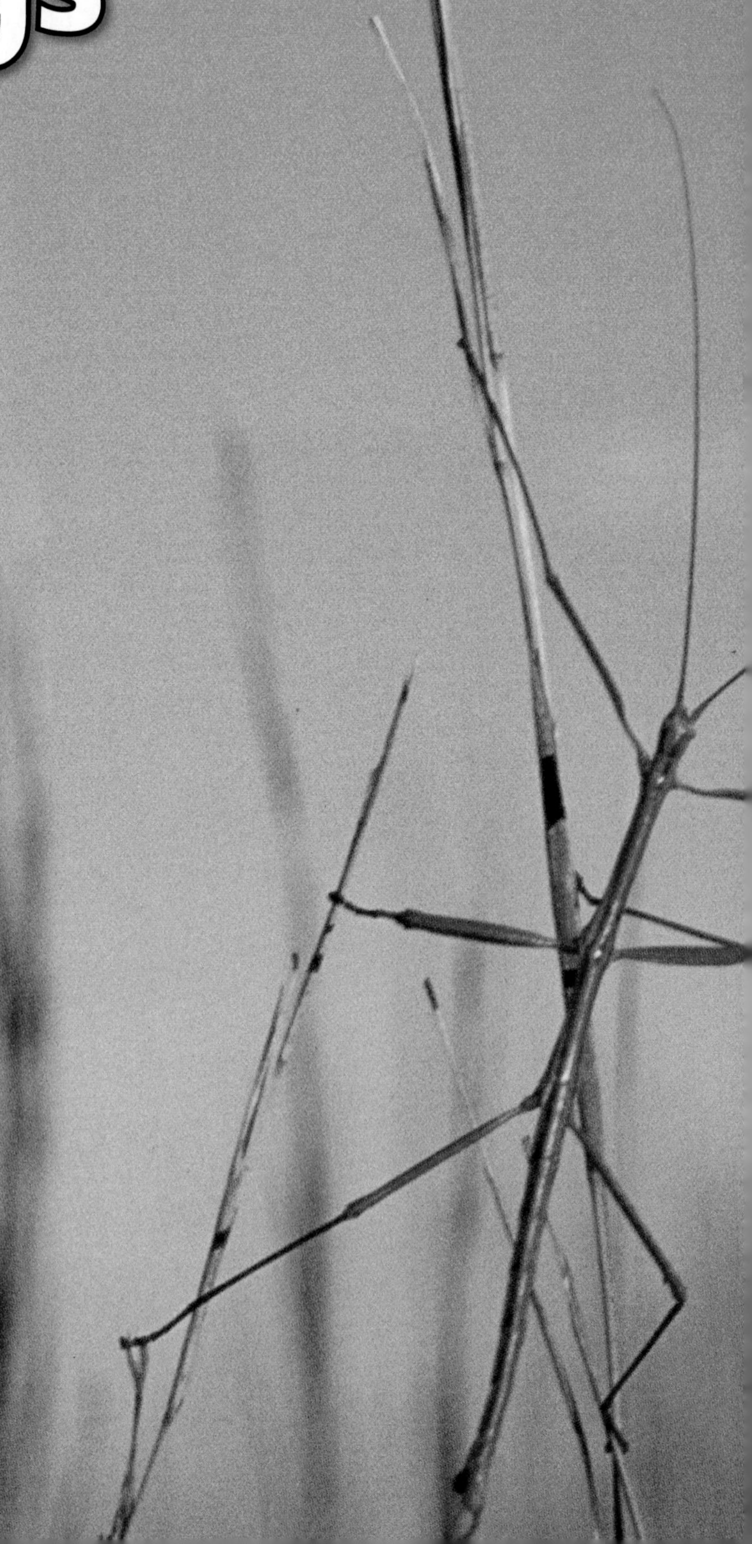

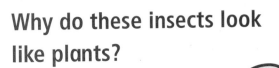

I wonder...

Why do these insects look
like plants?

What do YOU wonder?

1

What Is an Environment?

Few people have ever seen jaguars in the wild. They live where it is easy to hide. Communicate what you know about where animals live.

106

Where Animals Live

You need

- **animal picture cards**
- **crayons**

Step 1

Look at the cards.
Choose an animal you
know about.

Step 2

Draw the animal where
it lives.

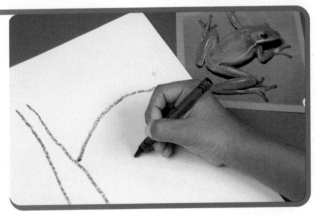

Step 3

Communicate with
classmates about what
you drew.

Inquiry Skill

When you **communicate**,
you tell about each thing
you drew in your picture.

VOCABULARY
environment

 READING FOCUS SKILL

MAIN IDEA AND DETAILS Look for the main ideas about environments.

Environments

An **environment** is made up of all the things in a place.

An environment has living things. It has plants and animals.

Find living and nonliving things in this environment.

An environment also has nonliving things, such as rocks and water.

⭐ (Focus Skill) **MAIN IDEA AND DETAILS**
What is an environment?

People and Environments

People can change environments. They may build houses and roads. They may make new things. People made many of the things you see in your environment.

 MAIN IDEA AND DETAILS How can people change environments?

Which things here did people make?
Which things were not made by people?

Focus Skill

1. MAIN IDEA AND DETAILS Copy and complete this chart.

Main Idea
An **Ⓐ** _____ is all the things in a place.

detail
People can **Ⓑ** _____ it.

detail
It has living things.

detail
It has **Ⓒ** _____ things.

2. SUMMARIZE Use the chart to write a lesson summary.

3. VOCABULARY Tell about this animal's **environment**.

Test Prep

4. Tell about some ways people can change their environments.

Links

Writing

Write a Description
Look at the environment outside your school. Write sentences about things you see that were made by people. Tell what each thing looks like. Tell what it is used for.

The slide was made by people. It is red and blue. It is for kids to play on.

For more links and activities, go to **www.hspscience.com**

What Helps Plants and Animals Live in Places?

Some Animals Hide

You need

- **colored paper clips**
- **colored paper**

Step 1

Put the clips on a sheet of colored paper. Which clips are hard to see?

Step 2

Put the clips on a sheet of paper of a different color. Which clips are hard to see now?

Step 3

Draw a conclusion about how color helps some animals hide.

Inquiry Skill

To **draw a conclusion** about animals' colors, think about the clips that were hard to see.

READING FOCUS SKILL

COMPARE AND CONTRAST Look for ways adaptations are alike and different.

Plant Adaptations

An **adaptation** is a body part or a behavior that helps a living thing.

Plants have adaptations. Some adaptations help them get water. A banyan tree has many roots. A jade plant has thick leaves that store water.

banyan tree

jade plant

Some adaptations help plants stay alive. Thorns on plants stop animals from eating them. Other adaptations help plants make new plants. Wings on maple seeds carry the seeds to new places. Flowers attract small animals. The animals help the plants make seeds.

maple seeds

COMPARE AND CONTRAST What are some plant adaptations? How are they alike and different?

hummingbird

rose

115

Animal Adaptations

Animals have adaptations, too. Some adaptations help animals eat. Sharp teeth help a lion bite meat. A long tongue helps an anteater get ants.

Some adaptations help animals move. Wings and feathers help a bird fly. Fins help a fish swim.

scarlet ibis

lion

anteater

Some adaptations keep animals safe. A porcupine has sharp quills. Other animals keep away from the quills.

Observe Beaks

Put crumbs from lunch on a tray. Put the tray outside where you can see it. Then watch for birds. What birds do you see? How does each one use its beak to eat?

 COMPARE AND CONTRAST
How are some animal adaptations alike?

goldfish

porcupine

117

Camouflage

Some animals have an adaptation called camouflage. **Camouflage** is a color or pattern that helps an animal hide. Animals need to hide to stay safe or to find food.

arctic fox in winter

arctic fox in summer

flounder

dead-leaf butterfly

frog

For more links and activities, go to
www.hspscience.com

Focus Skill

1. COMPARE AND CONTRAST Copy and complete this chart.

Adaptation

alike	different
A _____ help living things.	Some help plants get **B** _____.
	Some help plants stay alive or **C** _____.
	Some help animals **D** _____.
	Some help **E** _____ move.
	Some help animals stay **F** _____.

2. DRAW CONCLUSIONS Why do you think some animals have camouflage?

3. VOCABULARY Use the word **adaptation** to tell about this picture.

Test Prep

4. Which adaptation helps plants store water?

A. flowers
B. sharp teeth
C. thick leaves
D. thorns

Links

Math

Counting Teeth

Some animals have many teeth. Others do not. How many teeth do you have? Use a mirror to count. Use the data to make a class graph. Does everyone have the same number of teeth?

How Many Teeth?

20 teeth
19 teeth
18 teeth

0 1 2 3 4 5 6 7 8 9 10

For more links and activities, go to www.hspscience.com

How Do Plants and Animals Need Each Other?

Fast Fact

Flowers make food that bees eat. Bees carry pollen, which helps plants make new plants. What else can you observe about plants and animals?

Animals in a Tree

You need

- **hand lens**

Find a tree with your class. Observe it with a hand lens. Record what you see.

Step 2

Sit quietly and observe. Record what animals in your tree are doing.

Step 3

How did animals use the tree? Talk about what you observed.

Inquiry Skill

Use your senses to help you observe.

Reading in Science

VOCABULARY

oxygen
pollen
food chain

READING FOCUS SKILL

MAIN IDEA AND DETAILS Look for the main ideas about how animals use plants and help plants.

Animals Use Plants

Animals use plants to meet their needs. Some live in plants or use them to make homes. Plants are good places for animals to hide in, too.

heron hiding in grass

deer hiding behind trees

beaver building a dam

Some animals use plants for food. Animals need to breathe oxygen from the air. **Oxygen** is a kind of gas. Plants put oxygen into the air.

 MAIN IDEA AND DETAILS
What are three ways animals use plants?

elephants eating leaves

123

Animals Help Plants

Some animals help plants make new plants. They carry **pollen** from flower to flower. Pollen is a powder that flowers need to make seeds.

honey possum carrying pollen

butterfly carrying pollen

Some animals help plants by carrying seeds. They take seeds to new places. The seeds may grow into new plants there.

⭐ **Focus Skill** **MAIN IDEA AND DETAILS**
How can animals help plants make new plants?

squirrel carrying seeds

dog carrying seeds

Food Chain

Animals can be grouped by what they eat. Some animals eat plants. Some eat other animals. A **food chain** shows how animals and plants are linked.

⭐ **MAIN IDEA AND DETAILS**
What does a food chain show?

Last, a bear eats the fish.

Next, a rainbow trout eats the stonefly.

First, a stonefly eats part of a plant.

Focus Skill

1. MAIN IDEA AND DETAILS Copy and complete this chart.

Main Idea
Animals and plants need each other.

detail	detail	detail	detail
Animals eat **A** ____.	Animals carry **B** ____ from flower to flower.	Animals use plants for **C** ____.	Animals carry **D** ____ to new places.

2. SUMMARIZE Write two sentences to summarize the lesson.

3. VOCABULARY Use the word **pollen** to tell about this animal.

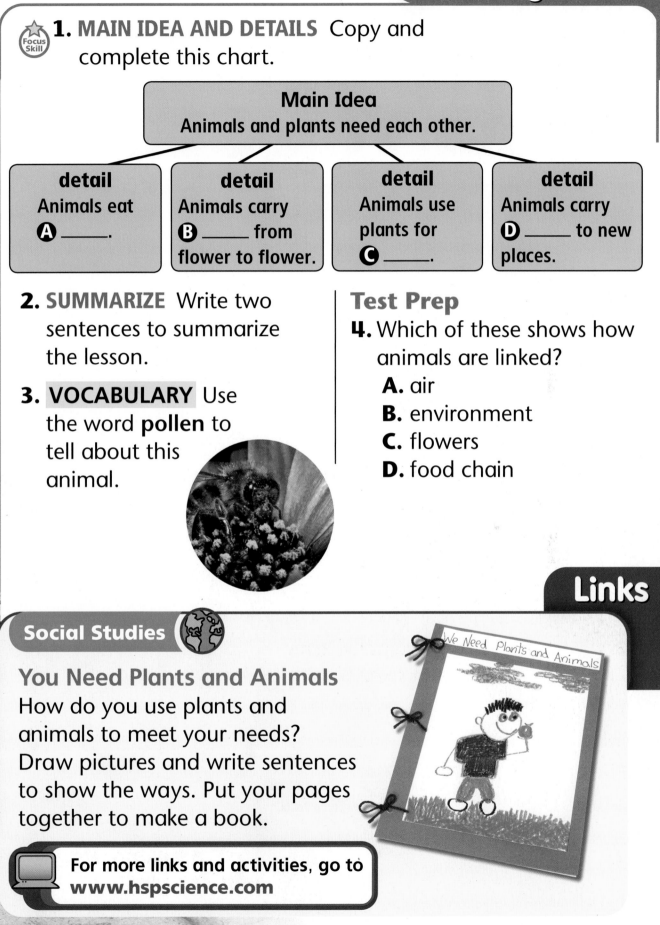

Test Prep

4. Which of these shows how animals are linked?
  A. air
  B. environment
  C. flowers
  D. food chain

Links

Social Studies

You Need Plants and Animals
How do you use plants and animals to meet your needs? Draw pictures and write sentences to show the ways. Put your pages together to make a book.

We Need Plants and Animals

For more links and activities, go to www.hspscience.com

SCIENCE *Spin* from WEEKLY READER®

Technology

Now You See It, Now You Don't

Do you ever wish you could hide like an arctic fox? Now your wish can come true.

Susumu Tachi is a teacher. He lives in Japan. Tachi made a coat to show how things can be hidden.

Tiny Glass Beads

The coat is covered by many tiny glass beads. The beads reflect light. Then you can see through a person wearing the coat.

THINK ABOUT IT
How is this coat similar to camouflage?

Seeing into the Future

Tachi says his idea might be used in many ways. Doctors could use tools with the beads on them. Then they could see through the tools when they operate.

Find out more! Log on to **www.hspscience.com**

129

Where Are All the Butterflies?

People often see monarch butterflies in the fall. The insects leave places in the north when the weather turns cold. They fly to warmer places in the south. Scientists want to know why.

Emma Griffiths helped scientists count butterflies. Emma helped by scooping up butterflies. Then scientists put a tiny tag on each insect. The tag showed other scientists that the butterflies came from Connecticut.

130

You Can Do It!

What Makes Seeds Stick?

Materials
- foam ball
- glue
- rough materials

What to Do

1. Find some seeds. Which ones might stick to animals?

2. Make a model of a seed that will stick to things.

3. Does your model stick to your clothes? How does this help you understand how seeds stick to animals?

Draw Conclusions

How is the ball a model of a seed that sticks to things?

Watch a Plant Change

Put two plants that are the same by a window. Mark one. Each day, turn the other plant. Do not turn the marked plant. After one week, how has the marked plant changed? Why did it do this?

Review and Test Preparation

Vocabulary Review

Choose the best word to complete each sentence.

environment p. 108   **oxygen** p. 123

camouflage p. 118   **pollen** p. 124

1. Powder from flowers is ____.

2. A gas that is part of air is ____.

3. An adaptation that helps an animal hide is ____.

4. A place that is made up of living and nonliving things is an ____.

Check Understanding

5. Name two animals. Tell how the adaptations of these animals are **alike**. Then tell how they are **different**.

6. How do plants help animals breathe?

    A. Plants put oxygen into the air.

    B. Animals eat plants.

    C. Plants store water.

    D. Animals can hide in plants.

Critical Thinking

7. Why do you think people change their environments? How do some changes harm the plants and animals that live there?

8. Look at these plants and animals. Draw them in order to show a food chain. Write about what happens.

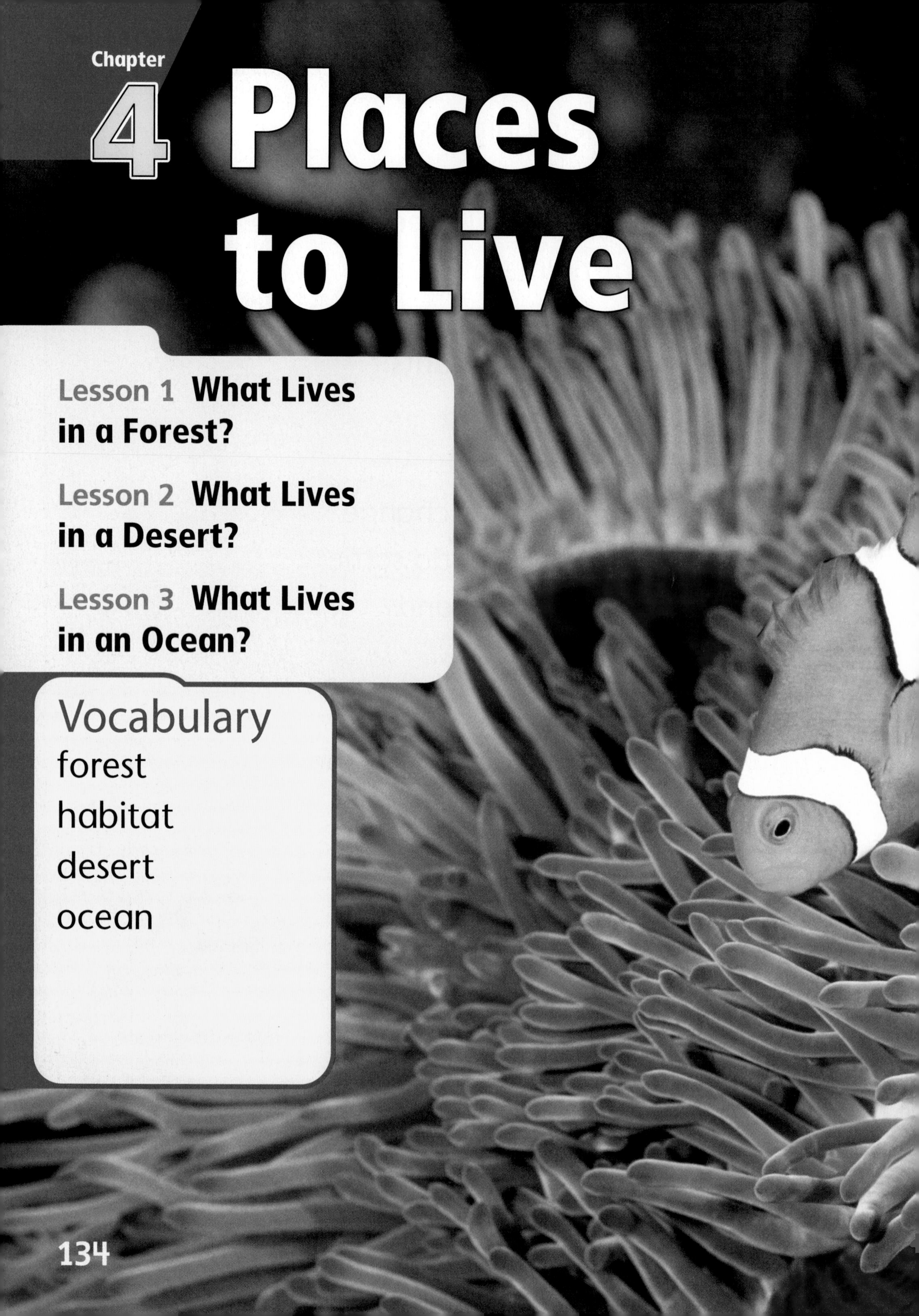

Chapter

4 Places to Live

Vocabulary

forest
habitat
desert
ocean

I wonder...

Why does this fish live here?

What do **YOU** wonder?

What Lives in a Forest?

Fast Fact

The trees in this redwood forest are the world's tallest living things. You can compare trees by size.

Compare Leaves and Bark

You need

- **dark-colored crayon**
- **paper**

Step 1

Go outside with your class. Find a leaf. Make a rubbing.

Step 2

Find the tree that the leaf is from. Make a rubbing of its bark.

Step 3

Compare your rubbings with a classmate's rubbings. Tell what you see.

Inquiry Skill

When you **compare**, you look for ways things are alike and ways they are different.

VOCABULARY
forest
habitat

READING FOCUS SKILL

MAIN IDEA AND DETAILS Look for the main ideas about forests.

Forests

A **forest** is land that is covered with trees. The trees shade the forest floor. The shade helps the soil stay moist.

MAIN IDEA AND DETAILS What is a forest?

Forest Plants

In a forest, trees get enough rain and warmth to grow tall. Their leaves can get the light they need. Ferns and flowers grow on the forest floor. They need water, but they do not need much light.

ferns

 MAIN IDEA AND DETAILS

How do trees get the light they need?

wildflowers

Insta-Lab

Made in the Shade

Wet two paper towels. Put them in a sunny place. Use a folder to make shade for one towel. Wait a few minutes. Then check the towels. Which one is wetter? How is the wetter towel like a forest floor?

Forest Animals

A forest has habitats for many animals. A **habitat** is a place where an animal finds food, water, and shelter. A bear needs a large part of a forest for its habitat. A smaller animal may need only a log.

MAIN IDEA AND DETAILS

What are some animals that may have habitats in a forest?

eagle

bear

skunk

How are these animals meeting their needs?

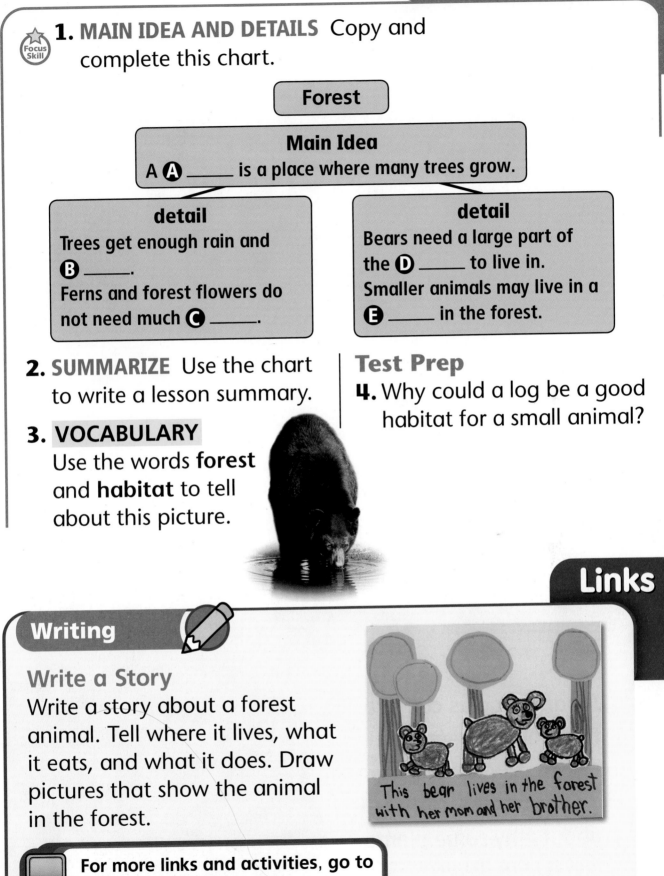

Focus Skill

1. MAIN IDEA AND DETAILS Copy and complete this chart.

Forest

Main Idea
A **Ⓐ** _____ is a place where many trees grow.

detail
Trees get enough rain and **Ⓑ** _____.
Ferns and forest flowers do not need much **Ⓒ** _____.

detail
Bears need a large part of the **Ⓓ** _____ to live in.
Smaller animals may live in a **Ⓔ** _____ in the forest.

2. SUMMARIZE Use the chart to write a lesson summary.

3. VOCABULARY
Use the words **forest** and **habitat** to tell about this picture.

Test Prep
4. Why could a log be a good habitat for a small animal?

Links

Writing

Write a Story
Write a story about a forest animal. Tell where it lives, what it eats, and what it does. Draw pictures that show the animal in the forest.

This bear lives in the forest with her mom and her brother.

For more links and activities, go to www.hspscience.com

What Lives in a Desert?

Fast Fact

A barrel cactus can live for almost 6 years on water stored in its stem. You can draw a conclusion about why some plants can live in deserts.

Desert Plants

You need

- 2 paper-towel leaf shapes
- water
- wax paper
- 2 paper clips

Make the leaf shapes damp. Fold the wax paper. Put one leaf inside the fold. Clip it.

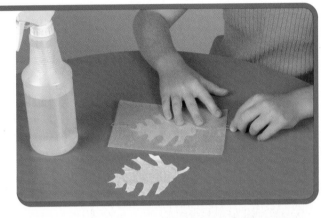

Put the leaf shapes in a sunny place. Observe them in one hour.

Which leaf was still damp? Why?
Draw a conclusion.

Inquiry Skill

Think about what you know about wax paper and water to **draw a conclusion**.

143

VOCABULARY
desert

⭐ **READING FOCUS SKILL**

MAIN IDEA AND DETAILS Look for the main ideas about deserts.

Deserts

A **desert** is land that gets very little rain. Most deserts are sunny all year long. The soil is very dry. Only some plants or animals can live there.

creosote

⭐ **MAIN IDEA AND DETAILS** How can you tell if a place is a desert?

Desert Plants

Desert plants do not need much water. A cactus is a desert plant. It can hold water in its thick stem. Its waxy covering helps keep water in.

MAIN IDEA AND DETAILS How does a cactus live without much water?

brittlebush

Insta-Lab

Soak It Up

Get a sponge that is very dry. Put water on it a little at a time. Observe the sponge. How does it change? How is the sponge like the stem of a cactus?

Desert Animals

Desert animals need to keep cool and find water. The dove and the hare rest in shady places. The tortoise gets water from its food.

MAIN IDEA AND DETAILS

What are important needs of desert animals?

desert hare

white-winged dove

How are these animals meeting their needs?

desert tortoise

Focus Skill

1. MAIN IDEA AND DETAILS Copy and complete this chart.

Desert

Main Idea
A desert is land that gets very little **A** _____.

detail
Desert plants do not need much **B** _____.
A cactus holds water in its **C** _____.

detail
Doves and hares rest in **D** _____ places to stay cool.
A **E** _____ gets water from the food it eats.

2. DRAW CONCLUSIONS Why are few plants and animals able to live in a desert?

3. VOCABULARY Use the word **desert** to tell about this picture.

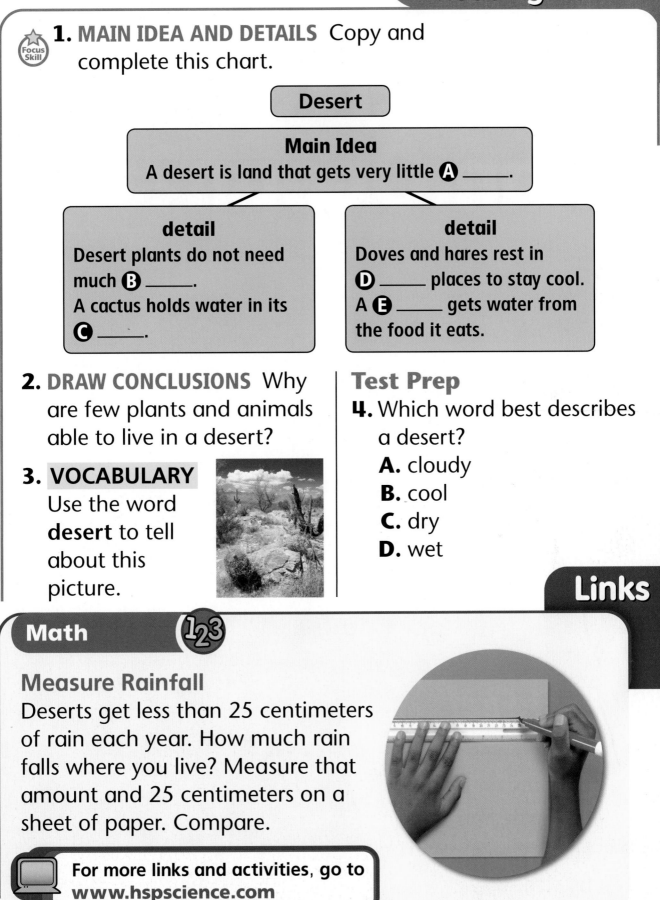

Test Prep

4. Which word best describes a desert?

　　A. cloudy
　　B. cool
　　C. dry
　　D. wet

Links

Math 123

Measure Rainfall
Deserts get less than 25 centimeters of rain each year. How much rain falls where you live? Measure that amount and 25 centimeters on a sheet of paper. Compare.

For more links and activities, go to **www.hspscience.com**

What Lives in an Ocean?

Fast Fact

Blue whales are the biggest animals on Earth. You can classify animals by size.

Animals in the Ocean

You need

- ocean animal picture cards

Observe the animals.
How are they alike?
How are they different?

Classify the animals
into groups.

Tell how the animals
in each group are
alike. Tell how the two
groups are different.

Inquiry Skill

When you classify
animals, you group them
by ways they are alike.

VOCABULARY
ocean

(Focus Skill) **READING FOCUS SKILL**

MAIN IDEA AND DETAILS Look for the main ideas about oceans.

Oceans

An **ocean** is a large body of salt water. Oceans cover much of Earth.

Ocean animals live where they can find food. Crabs find their food near the shore.

goatfish

hermit crab

Some ocean animals swim to find their food. Fish, stingrays, and sea turtles may swim hundreds of miles.

Focus Skill **MAIN IDEA AND DETAILS**
Where do ocean animals live?

stingray

sea turtle

Insta-Lab

Bones and Cartilage
Fish have bones. Rays have cartilage. Feel your wrist. It has bones. Feel your ear. It has cartilage. How are bones and cartilage alike? How are they different?

A Coral Reef

Corals are very small animals. They form coral reefs. Many other animals find food and shelter on the reefs.

sea fan coral

sea whip coral

candy cane coral

For more links and activities, go to
www.hspscience.com

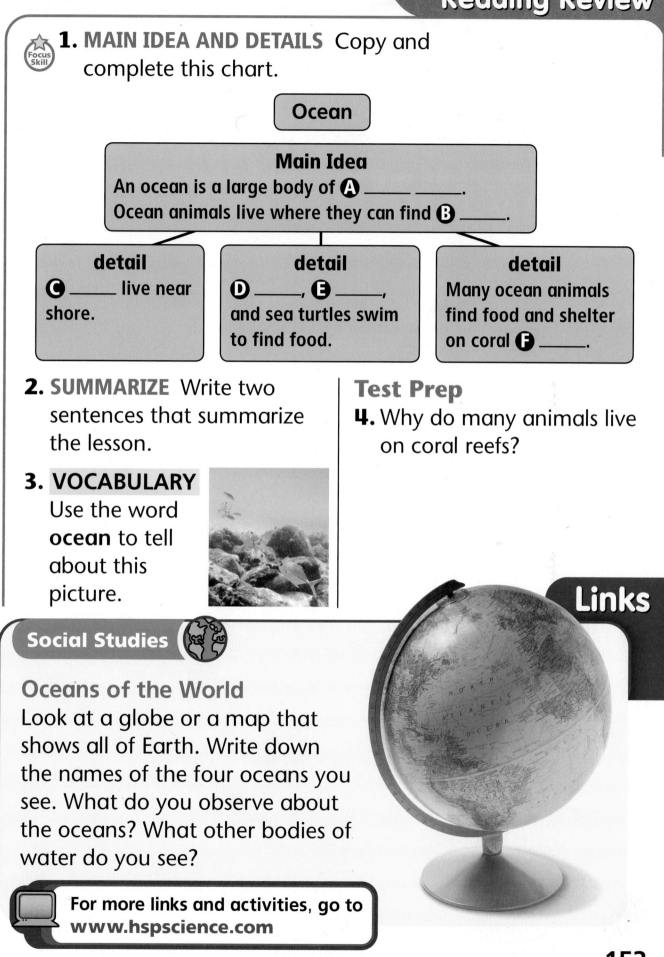

Focus Skill

1. MAIN IDEA AND DETAILS Copy and complete this chart.

Ocean

Main Idea
An ocean is a large body of **A** _____ _____.
Ocean animals live where they can find **B** _____.

detail
C _____ live near shore.

detail
D _____, **E** _____, and sea turtles swim to find food.

detail
Many ocean animals find food and shelter on coral **F** _____.

2. SUMMARIZE Write two sentences that summarize the lesson.

3. VOCABULARY Use the word **ocean** to tell about this picture.

Test Prep

4. Why do many animals live on coral reefs?

Links

Social Studies

Oceans of the World
Look at a globe or a map that shows all of Earth. Write down the names of the four oceans you see. What do you observe about the oceans? What other bodies of water do you see?

For more links and activities, go to **www.hspscience.com**

A New Plane Fights Fires

Wildfires burn large parts of forests in the western United States. Wildfires can move quickly. This can put firefighters in danger.

Now firefighters have a new tool to help them. This tool is a robot plane called Altus II.

Plane Without a Pilot

Altus II is 17 meters (55 feet) across. It can fly at about 185 kilometers (115 miles) per hour. The plane does not have a pilot. It is controlled by people on the ground.

The Altus II has cameras on board. It takes pictures of fires. The cameras can see through smoke. They can also see places that might catch fire.

The plane can also be used by people to keep track of floods or hurricanes.

THINK ABOUT IT
How does using Altus II help firefighters?

All in a Day's Work

The Altus II is light. It does not need much fuel. It can fly for up to 24 hours at a time.

Find out more! Log on to
www.hspscience.com

A Walk in the Woods

What lives in a forest? Andrew Seto found out when his class went for a walk in the woods near his school.

Andrew knows that plants live in a forest. He saw an oak tree and a fern.

Andrew knows that birds make their homes in trees. He saw that squirrels make their homes in trees, too.

Fish Habitat

What to Do

Materials
- fishbowl with water
- aquarium rocks
- fish

1. Put rocks in the bottom of a fishbowl or an aquarium. Fill it with water. Put in two or more fish.

2. Feed the fish every day. Keep the habitat clean.

3. Observe and record what you see each day.

Draw Conclusions

How is this habitat different from an ocean?

Deserts Around the World

Find pictures of deserts in other parts of the world. Observe the land and the plants and animals that live there. How are these deserts like American deserts? How are they different? Draw pictures to show what you find out. Write about them.

Camels live in deserts in the Middle East.

Review and Test Preparation

Vocabulary Review

Use the words below to complete the sentences.

forest p. 138   desert p. 144

habitat p. 140   ocean p. 150

1. A large body of salt water is called an ____.

2. A place where an animal can find food, water, and shelter is a ____.

3. Land that is covered with trees is a ____.

4. Land that gets little rain is a ____.

Check Understanding

5. Compare these animals' habitats.

6. Why is a coral reef a good habitat for this eel?

    A. A coral reef is very dry.

    B. The eel can live without much water.

    C. The eel needs shade.

    D. The eel can find food and shelter.

Critical Thinking

7. Read the clues. Name the plant or animal. Tell where it lives.

This plant needs rain and warmth to grow. It grows tall so that its leaves can get light.

8. Write clues about a plant or animal from this chapter. Ask a partner to name your plant or animal.

About Our Earth

The Grand Canyon

TO: daisy@hspscience.com

FROM: oscar@hspscience.com

RE: Grand Canyon, Arizona

Dear Daisy,

I visited the Grand Canyon. It is a long way down to the bottom. Do you know how it was formed?

Write back soon.

Oscar

TO: maya@hspscience.com

FROM: devon@hspscience.com

RE: Hazelton, Pennsylvania

Dear Maya,

I went to visit my grandfather's farm. We dug a deep hole to plant a tree. The soil was a different color at the bottom of the hole.

Write back soon.

Devon

Experiment!

Plants and Soil

As you do this unit, you will find out about the earth. Plan and do a test. See if plants change the amount of soil that is washed away by water.

5 Our Earth

Lesson 1 What Are Some Kinds of Land?

Lesson 2 What Are Some Kinds of Water?

Lesson 3 How Does Earth Change?

Vocabulary

mountain	river
hill	lake
valley	ocean
plain	flood
beach	drought
stream	erosion

I wonder...

How much water flows over Niagara Falls each day?

What do **you** wonder?

What Are Some Kinds of Land?

Fast Fact

Mt. McKinley, in Alaska, is our country's highest mountain. You can classify land by height, shape, and where it is.

164

Kinds of Land

You need

- **land picture cards**

Step 1

Look at the pictures. Tell how they are alike and how they are different.

Step 2

Classify the picture cards. Group pictures by the kinds of land they show.

Step 3

Talk about the groups you made.

Inquiry Skill

You can **classify** land by its shape and by where it is.

VOCABULARY

mountain   plain
hill   beach
valley

READING FOCUS SKILL

COMPARE AND CONTRAST Read to find out how kinds of land can be alike and different.

Mountains and Hills

Land on Earth has different shapes. One land shape is a mountain. A **mountain** is the highest kind of land. It has sides that slope up to a top. Some mountains have rocky peaks. Others are round on top.

mountain

A **hill** is a high place that is smaller than a mountain. Most hills are round on top.

Focus Skill **COMPARE AND CONTRAST** How are mountains and hills alike?

hills

Valleys and Plains

   Valleys and plains are lower lands.
A **valley** is low land between
mountains or hills. A **plain** is flat land
that spreads out a long way.

⭐ (Focus Skill) **COMPARE AND CONTRAST** How are valleys
and plains different?

valley

plain

Insta-Lab

Model Land

Use clay or damp sand to model kinds of land. Work with a partner. Show a mountain, a hill, a valley, and a plain. Label each land shape.

Beaches

In some places, a lake or an ocean has a beach. A **beach** is flat, sandy land along a shore. Some beaches can also be rocky.

 COMPARE AND CONTRAST How is a beach different from other kinds of land?

beach

1. COMPARE AND CONTRAST Copy and complete this chart.

Earth's Land

alike

All are high lands.

All are low lands.

different

A **A** _____ is the highest kind of land.
A **B** _____ is a high place that is smaller than a mountain.

A **C** _____ is low land between mountains.
A **D** _____ is flat land that spreads out a long way.
A **E** _____ is flat, sandy land along a shore.

2. SUMMARIZE Use the chart to write a lesson summary.

3. VOCABULARY Write a sentence to tell how **plains** and **mountains** are different.

Test Prep

4. Which of these is flat, sandy land along a shore?
  A. beach
  B. hill
  C. mountain
  D. valley

Links

Writing

Essay
Choose a kind of land you would like to visit. Write about why you want to go and what you would do there. Then draw a picture of yourself in that place.

For more links and activities, go to **www.hspscience.com**

I would like to go to the mountains.

What Are Some Kinds of Water?

Fast Fact

This river has been flowing over these rocks for millions of years. You can infer how water and land are different.

172

Explore Land and Water

You need

• **globe**

Step 1

Observe the globe.
What can you see?

Step 2

Find land. Then find
water. How do you know
the difference?

Step 3

Infer how Earth's land
and water are different.

Inquiry Skill

Use what you observed to
infer how land and water
are different.

VOCABULARY
stream
river
lake
ocean

⭐ **READING FOCUS SKILL**

COMPARE AND CONTRAST Look for ways bodies of water are alike and ways they are different.

Streams, Rivers, and Lakes

Streams, rivers, and lakes are bodies of fresh water. A **stream** is a small body of moving water. Streams may begin in mountains. The water flows downhill. The streams flow together into a river. A **river** is a large body of moving water.

stream

river

lake

Rivers flow together. Rivers may flow into lakes and oceans. A **lake** is a still body of water with land all around it.

 COMPARE AND CONTRAST How are rivers and streams alike?

Insta-Lab

Moving Water

Cut a cardboard tube in half the long way. Put the halves on a tray. Put something under one end of one half. Pour water into each half. Observe. Infer how the land's shape makes rivers flow quickly or slowly.

Oceans

An **ocean** is a large body of salty water. Most of Earth's water is in oceans.

 COMPARE AND CONTRAST How are oceans different from other bodies of water?

ocean

1. COMPARE AND CONTRAST Copy and complete this chart.

Earth's Water

alike

different

All are kinds of water.

A **A** _____ is a small body of moving water.
A **B** _____ is a large body of moving water.
A **C** _____ is a still body of water with land all around it.
An **D** _____ is a large body of salty water.

2. DRAW CONCLUSIONS Tell whether a river will flow faster down a steep hill or a gentle hill.

3. VOCABULARY Tell how you know this is a **river**.

Test Prep

4. How are streams, rivers, and lakes alike?

Links

Math

Model Fractions
Draw a circle. Divide it into 4 equal parts. Color 3 parts blue and 1 part brown. What does this show about the water and land on Earth? Write a fraction.

For more links and activities, go to www.hspscience.com

How Does Earth Change?

Model Erosion

You need

- damp soil
- tray
- water

Step 1

Use soil to **make a model** of a mountain.

Step 2

Slowly pour water onto the top of the mountain.

Step 3

Observe. How does the mountain change? Tell how the **model** shows how water changes real mountains.

Inquiry Skill

Some changes take a long time. You can **make a model** to see how the changes happen.

READING FOCUS SKILL

CAUSE AND EFFECT Look for ways that water can change Earth.

Weather Changes Earth

Heavy rains may cause a flood. A **flood** happens when rivers and streams get too full. The water flows onto land. A flood may carry soil to a new place.

flood

This is the same place during a drought.

Dry weather may cause a drought. A **drought** is a long time with less rain than usual. The land gets very dry. Plants may die.

⭐ Focus Skill

CAUSE AND EFFECT
What can weather do to Earth's land?

Insta-Lab

Flooding
Fill two trays with dry soil. Slowly pour 1 cup of water onto one tray. Then quickly pour 1 cup of water onto the other tray. What happens? Infer why some rains cause floods and others do not.

The Grand Canyon

Moving water changes the land. It carries rocks and soil to new places. This is called **erosion**. Erosion formed the Grand Canyon over millions of years.

1. A long time ago, water began to flow over the land.

2. The moving water carried away soil and rocks.

3. The water's path became very deep. In time, it formed the Grand Canyon.

For more links and activities, go to www.hspscience.com

Focus Skill

1. CAUSE AND EFFECT Copy and complete this chart.

Earth Changes

cause	effect
Heavy rain falls. →	There may be a **Ⓐ** _____.
No rain falls. →	There may be a **Ⓑ** _____.
Water moves over land. →	It carries away **Ⓒ** _____ and **Ⓓ** _____ to new places.

2. SUMMARIZE Use the chart to write a summary of this lesson.

3. VOCABULARY Use the word **erosion** to talk about this picture.

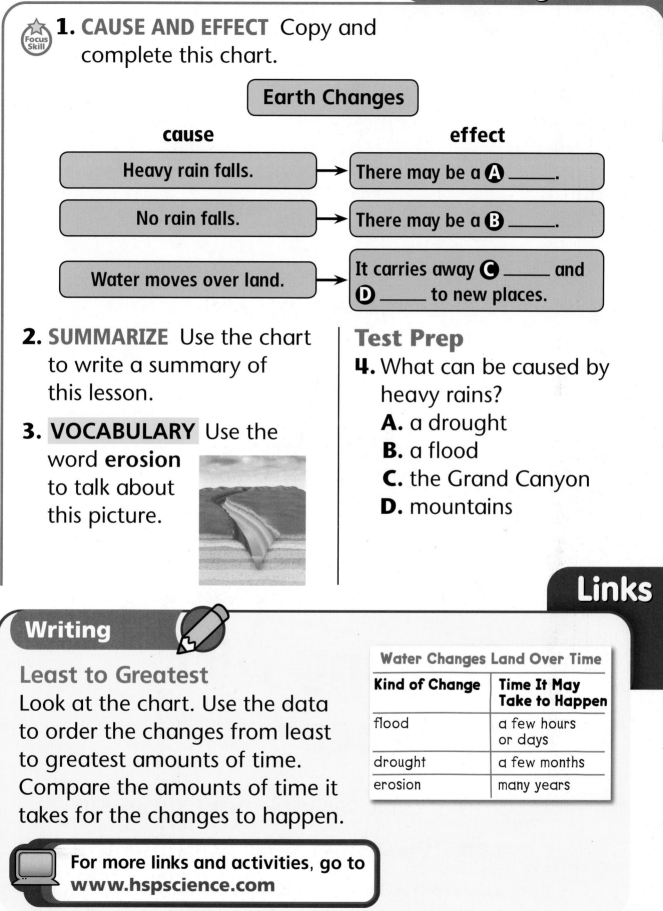

Test Prep

4. What can be caused by heavy rains?
- **A.** a drought
- **B.** a flood
- **C.** the Grand Canyon
- **D.** mountains

Links

Writing

Least to Greatest

Look at the chart. Use the data to order the changes from least to greatest amounts of time. Compare the amounts of time it takes for the changes to happen.

Water Changes Land Over Time	
Kind of Change	**Time It May Take to Happen**
flood	a few hours or days
drought	a few months
erosion	many years

For more links and activities, go to **www.hspscience.com**

Holding Dirt in Place

Take a closer look next time you drive by a work site. Look for the low, black material that looks like a fence.

That material is called a silt fence. Workers often dig up dirt, soil, and plants when they work on a road. The loose soil might wash away when it rains. Silt fences hold the loose soil in place.

When the work is finished, workers put the soil into places that need it. That way they save the soil and keep streams from clogging.

Don't Fence Me In

Silt fences are made of a special material that holds the soil but lets the water run through.

THINK ABOUT IT

How do trees and plants keep dirt from washing away?

Find out more! Log on to
www.hspscience.com

Stopping Erosion

Nina Rojas knows that trees give shade on a hot day. She also knows that trees can stop soil from washing away. "Planting trees and plants helps stop erosion," thought Nina. So she planted trees near a river in her city.

Nina knows those trees will help keep the soil in place. They will also make the park a prettier place to visit.

186

You Can Do It!

Explore Salt Water

What to Do

1. What happens to objects in fresh water? What happens to them in salt water? Make predictions.
2. Put the carrot in the water. Observe.
3. Add salt to the water. Stop when you see a change.

Materials
- water
- carrot
- salt

Draw Conclusions

What happens to objects that are placed in salt water?

What Does Moving Water Carry?

What can moving water carry away? With a grown-up's help, get a cup of water from a stream or river. Pour the water through a paper filter. Use a hand lens to observe. What is left in the filter?

Stream Water

Review and Test Preparation

Vocabulary Review

Tell which picture goes best with each word.

1. **mountain** p. 166
2. **plain** p. 168
3. **beach** p. 170
4. **stream** p. 174
5. **lake** p. 175
6. **flood** p. 180

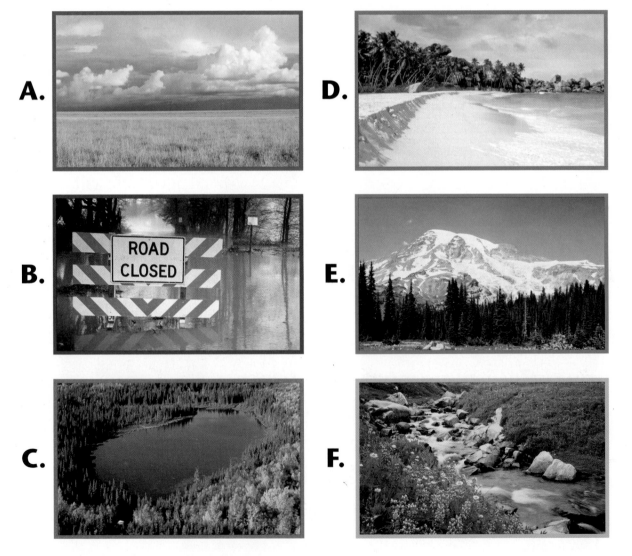

A.

B.
ROAD CLOSED

C.

D.

E.

F.

Check Understanding

7. Copy and complete this chart.

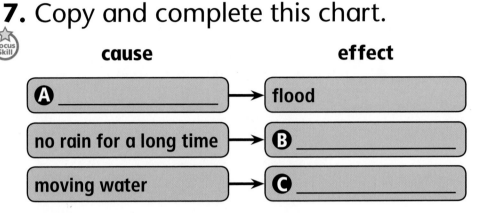

8. Where is most of Earth's water?

  A. in floods

  B. in lakes

  C. in oceans

  D. in rivers

Critical Thinking

9. Put these kinds of land in order from highest to lowest. Tell how you know.

A.   **B.**   **C.**

10. Some people work to stop erosion. Why do you think they do this?

Lesson 1 What Are Natural Resources?

Lesson 2 What Can We Observe About Rocks and Soil?

Lesson 3 How Can We Protect Natural Resources?

Vocabulary

natural resource

rock

soil

humus

pollution

reduce

reuse

recycle

I wonder…

Where does water come from?

What do you wonder?

What Are Natural Resources?

Fast Fact

Long ago, people used moving air, or wind, to travel in sailing ships. You can observe ways people use natural resources.

All Around You

You need

● crayons

● construction paper

Step 1

Make a chart like this one.

Things I Saw Outdoors	
animals	plants
water	land

Step 2

Go outside. **Observe** everything around you. Draw and label the things that belong in the chart.

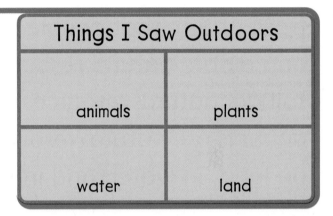

Step 3

Share your chart with a classmate. Did you both **observe** the same things?

Inquiry Skill

When you **observe**, you use your senses to find out about things.

193

VOCABULARY

natural
  resource

 READING FOCUS SKILL

MAIN IDEA AND DETAILS Look for the main ideas about natural resources.

Natural Resources

A **natural resource** is anything from nature that people can use. Water and air are natural resources. Rocks and soil are natural resources. Plants and animals are natural resources that live on land, in water, and in air.

MAIN IDEA AND DETAILS
What is a natural resource?

What natural resources do you see in this picture?

How are these people using water?

Water

Water is a natural resource that all living things need. People drink water and use it to clean and to cook. People travel on water, too.

⭐ Focus Skill **MAIN IDEA AND DETAILS**
What are some ways people use water?

Insta-Lab

Can Water Cool You?

Wrap one thermometer in a damp towel. Wrap another in a dry towel. Check them after 10 minutes. Which is cooler? How can you use water to keep your body cool?

Air

Air is a natural resource. You can not see air, but it is all around you. Many living things need air to live. People and many animals breathe air. People use air to fill things such as balloons. They also use air to make things move.

⭐ **MAIN IDEA AND DETAILS** What are some ways people use air?

How are these people using air?

Focus Skill

1. MAIN IDEA AND DETAILS Copy and complete this chart.

Main Idea
A **(A)** _____ is anything from nature that people can use.

detail	detail	detail
People use **(B)** _____ for drinking, cleaning, and cooking.	People and many animals breathe **(C)** _____.	Plants, animals, rocks, and soil are some other natural resources.

2. DRAW CONCLUSIONS Is everything that people use a natural resource? Explain.

3. VOCABULARY Use the words **natural resource** to talk about this picture.

Test Prep
4. How do people use air?
  A. They drink it.
  B. They build with it.
  C. They clean with it.
  D. They breathe it.

Links

Writing

Water Poem
Make a list of sounds that water can make. Use your list to write a poem about water. Draw a picture.

Bath Time
I get in the water — splish, splash, splish!
Soon I'm splashing like a fish.

For more links and activities, go to www.hspscience.com

What Can We Observe About Rocks and Soil?

Fast Fact

Farm walls are often made with rocks found in the farm's fields. One way to classify rocks is by where they are found.

Classify Rocks

You need

- **hand lens**

- **rocks**

Use a hand lens to observe each rock.

Sort the rocks by grouping those that are the same. Make a chart to show how you **classified** the rocks.

Rocks			
White			

Use the chart to tell how the rocks are alike. Then tell how they are different.

Inquiry Skill

You **classify** things by the ways they are alike.

VOCABULARY
rock
soil
humus

READING FOCUS SKILL

COMPARE AND CONTRAST Look for ways rocks and kinds of soil are alike. Also look for ways they are different.

Rocks

A **rock** is a hard, nonliving thing that comes from Earth. Rocks are a natural resource.

The walls of this building are made of rock.

People use rocks in different ways. They build with rocks. They carve some rocks into statues. Some things from rocks, such as salt, are in the food you eat.

COMPARE AND CONTRAST
Compare some ways people use rocks.

Pretzels have salt on them. People get salt from rocks.

This statue is made of a kind of rock called marble.

Soil

The top layer of Earth is **soil**. Soil is made up of clay, sand, and humus. Clay and sand are small pieces of rock. **Humus** is pieces of dead plants and animals. Soil in different places may have different amounts of sand, humus, and clay.

sand

+

humus

+

clay

=

soil

Soil is a natural resource. Some kinds can hold more water. People use soil to grow plants for food. Plants take water and other things they need from soil.

A girl plants seeds in soil.

COMPARE AND CONTRAST
How are kinds of soil alike and different?

Insta-Lab

Hold It!
Put a coffee filter on a cup. Hold it in place with a rubber band. Put soil on the filter. Pour $\frac{1}{2}$ cup of water onto the soil. Measure the water that passes through into the cup. How much water did the soil hold?

203

Other Things in Soil

Different things may be in soil. Worms and other animals may live there. Plant roots grow down into soil. Pieces of dead plants and animals may be in soil. Small rocks may be in it, too.

Focus Skill **COMPARE AND CONTRAST** Compare some of the different things found in soil.

dead plant

roots

worm

rock

204

1. COMPARE AND CONTRAST Copy and complete this chart.

Focus Skill

Rocks and Soil

alike

All are hard, nonliving things that come from **A** _____.

Soil is made up of sand, **C** _____, and clay.

different

People use rocks to build, to carve into **B** _____, and to use in food.

Different things, such as, roots and rocks, may be in soil.

2. SUMMARIZE Use the chart to write a summary of the lesson.

3. VOCABULARY Use the words **rock** and **soil** to tell about this picture.

Test Prep

4. Why are rocks and soil natural resources?

Links

Math ①②③

Compare Rock and Soil Masses

Get $\frac{1}{2}$ cup of soil and $\frac{1}{2}$ cup of small rocks. Use a balance to compare their masses. Then draw pictures and write >, <, or = to show what you found out.

For more links and activities, go to www.hspscience.com

How Can We Protect Natural Resources?

Fast Fact

Some of the things on playgrounds are made from recycled plastic jugs! You can draw a conclusion about why people should recycle things.

What Happens to Trash?

You need

- lettuce
- napkin
- piece of foam cup
- pan of soil

Step 1

Bury the lettuce, the napkin, and the piece of foam cup in the soil.

Step 2

Water the soil every three days. After two weeks, dig up the things. What do you **observe**?

Step 3

Draw a conclusion. How could trash harm the land? Why?

Inquiry Skill

Use what you observe and what you know to draw a conclusion.

VOCABULARY

pollution
reduce
reuse
recycle

Focus Skill **READING FOCUS SKILL**

CAUSE AND EFFECT Look for ways people can take care of natural resources.

Taking Care of Resources

Pollution harms our natural resources. **Pollution** is waste that causes harm to land, water, and air. Pollution also causes harm to plants and animals.

People can pick up trash on land.

People can help take care of natural resources. They can put trash in its place. They can clean up trash. They can also walk or ride bikes instead of using cars. Cars and trucks make air pollution and use natural resources.

⭐ **CAUSE AND EFFECT** What does pollution cause?

People can walk instead of using cars.

People can pick up trash in water.

Reduce, Reuse, Recycle

People can help care for natural resources. They can reduce, reuse, and recycle. This makes less trash. It also helps save natural resources.

To **reduce** something means to use less of it. People can use cloth bags. This reduces the number of paper and plastic bags that are used.

To **reuse** means to use something again. People can reuse food jars. The jars can hold pencils and other things.

To **recycle** means to use old things to make new things. People can recycle newpapers. The old papers can be made into new paper.

⭐ **CAUSE AND EFFECT** What effect does recycling have on the amount of trash?

Insta-Lab

Reuse an Egg Carton
Decorate an egg carton. Use it to store things you collect. You can keep different kinds of things in the different cups.

Ways to Save Resources

This family is saving resources.
How is each family member helping?

Turn off the lights when you leave a room.

Turn off the water when you do not need it.

Turn down the heat. Put on a sweater to stay warm.

Recycle.

For more links and activities, go to
www.hspscience.com

Focus Skill

1. CAUSE AND EFFECT Copy and complete this chart.

Natural Resources

cause	effect
People make pollution.	Pollution harms our **Ⓐ** _____.
People clean up **Ⓑ** _____.	People take care of resources.
People **Ⓒ** _____, reuse, and recycle.	People make less **Ⓓ** _____.

2. DRAW CONCLUSIONS
How can you take care of resources at your home?

3. VOCABULARY Use the word **pollution** to talk about this picture.

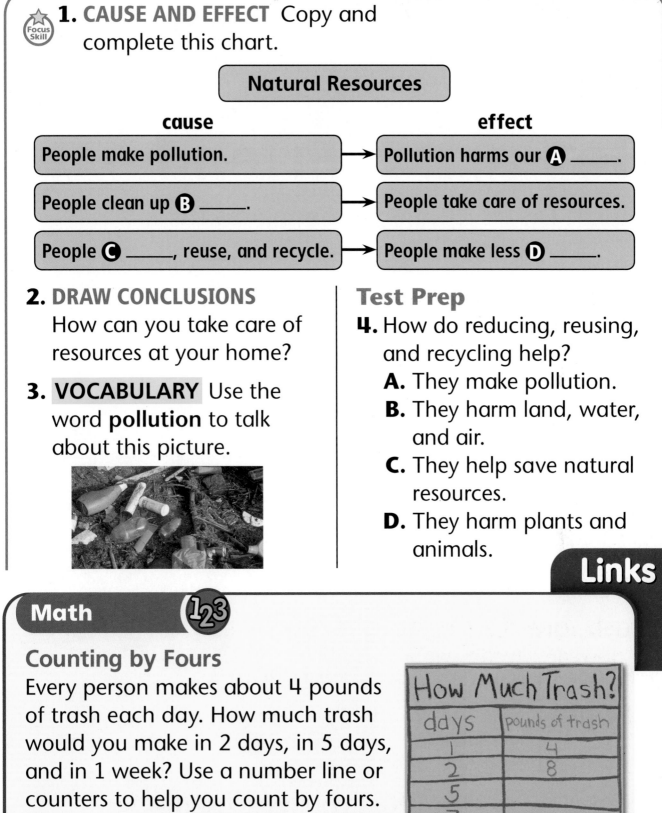

Test Prep

4. How do reducing, reusing, and recycling help?

A. They make pollution.

B. They harm land, water, and air.

C. They help save natural resources.

D. They harm plants and animals.

Links

Math 1₂3

Counting by Fours

Every person makes about 4 pounds of trash each day. How much trash would you make in 2 days, in 5 days, and in 1 week? Use a number line or counters to help you count by fours. Show your work in a chart.

How Much Trash?

days	pounds of trash
1	4
2	8
5	
7	

For more links and activities, go to **www.hspscience.com**

Be Earth's Friend

Earth Day is a time for people to think about taking care of Earth. People can keep plants and animals healthy. They can also help keep Earth clean.

1. Reduce.

Each person in the United States makes about 2 kilograms (4 pounds) of trash every day! So landfills, or places where people dump trash, are starting to get full.

People should reduce the amount of trash they throw away.

2. Reuse.

Some trash in landfills could be used for other things! People should find more ways to reuse trash.

3. Recycle.

Paper takes up the largest amount of space in most landfills. Paper can be easily recycled.

People can recycle by taking old newspapers to a recycling center.

4. Respect.

Many times people forget to respect, or care for, Earth. One way to show respect for Earth is to use fewer resources.

Respect Earth by turning off the water while you brush your teeth.

THINK ABOUT IT

What does Earth Day teach people about natural resources?

Find out more! Log on to
www.hspscience.com

Studying Rivers

Dr. Ruth Patrick is a nature scientist. Her father taught her to love plants, streams, and rivers.

Dr. Patrick looks at how pollution can hurt a river. Dr. Patrick studies the plants and animals that live in rivers. She makes a list of things scientists can check to see if a river is polluted. Dr. Patrick helps keep our rivers clean.

Making Water Clean

What to Do

1. Mix salt in water. Taste it. Pour it into the tub.

2. Put the other cup inside the tub. Cover the tub. Use the rubber band to hold the plastic in place. Put marbles on top.

3. Put the tub in the sun for two hours. Then take out the cup. Taste the water.

Materials
- salt
- 2 cups
- water
- spoon
- tub of sand
- plastic wrap
- rubber band
- 3 marbles

Draw Conclusions
What do you think happened to the water?

Too Much Packaging

Some foods come in packages that make lots of trash. Look at foods in your kitchen. Draw those that have too much packaging. Then draw to show how these foods could have less packaging.

Juice boxes have too much packaging. You could buy jars of juice.

Review and Test Preparation

Vocabulary Review

Tell which picture goes best with each word or words.

1. natural resource
p. 194

A.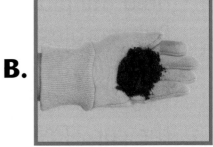

2. rock p. 200

B.

3. humus p. 202

C.

4. recycle p. 211

D.

Check Understanding

5. Tell the **details** about the natural resources in this picture.

6. Which part of soil is pieces of dead plants and animals?

   A. clay

   B. humus

   C. rock

   D. soil

7. Which of these harms natural resources?

   F. air   **H.** pollution

   G. humus   **J.** recycling

Critical Thinking

8. You want to take care of resources in your school. Write a plan. Tell each thing you would do. Tell why each thing would help.

UNIT D

EARTH SCIENCE

Weather, Seasons, and the Sky

Spring Maple-Sugaring Festival

TO: colton@hspscience.com

FROM: emily@hspscience.com

RE: Massachusetts

Dear Colton,

I got to see how maple syrup is made. In the spring, sap is collected from the trees and is boiled. It tastes good on pancakes!

Emily

220

North Country Planetarium

TO: stan@hspscience.com

FROM: mike@hspscience.com

RE: Plattsburgh State University

Dear Stan,

I saw the moon and the stars. I was not outside. I was inside a planetarium. Do you like to look for objects in the sky?

Your friend,

Mike

Starry, Starry Night

As you do this unit, you will find out about objects in the sky. Plan and do a test. Find out how the nighttime sky is different from the daytime sky.

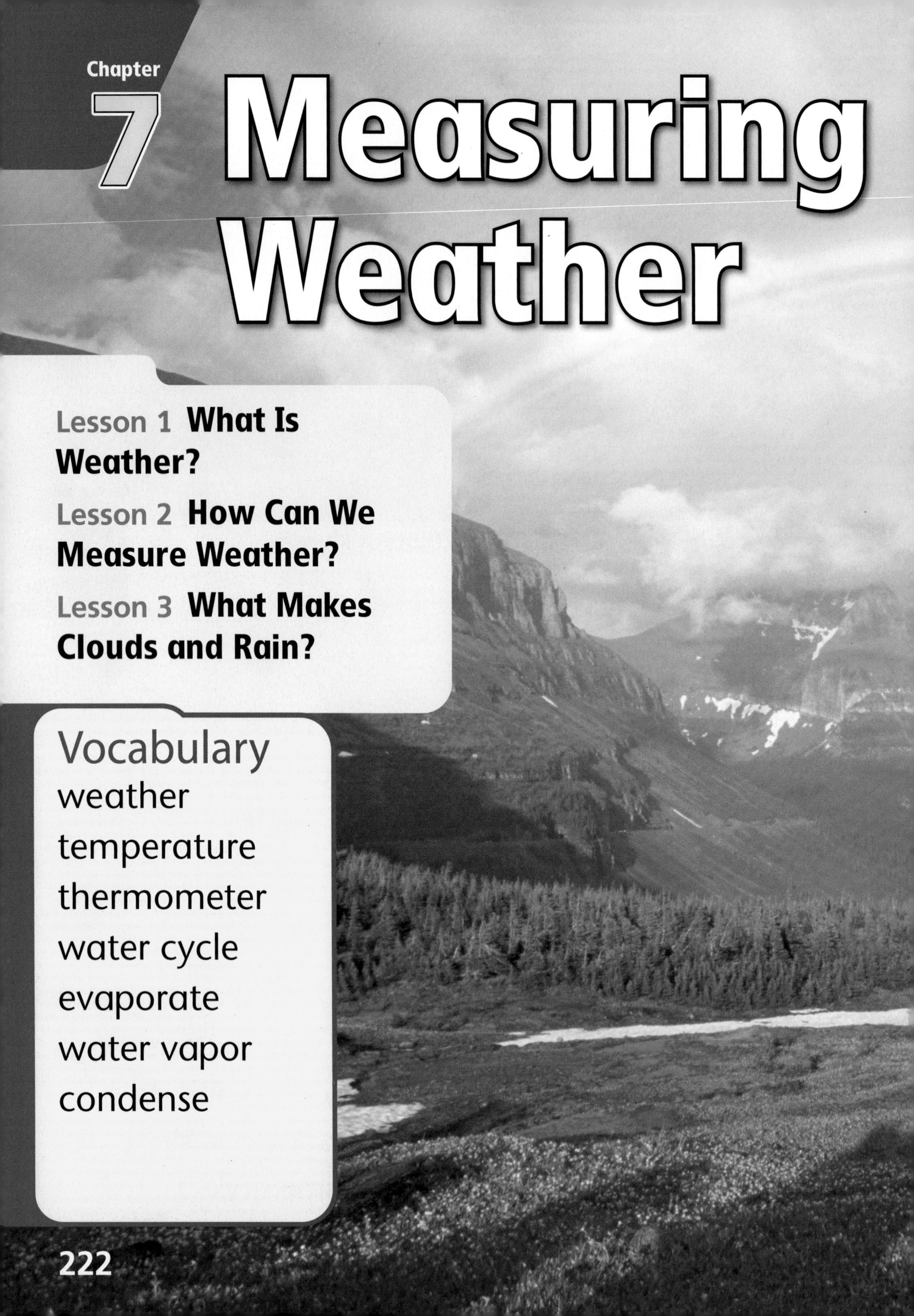

Chapter 7

Measuring Weather

Vocabulary

weather
temperature
thermometer
water cycle
evaporate
water vapor
condense

I wonder...

What makes a rainbow?

What do **YOU** wonder?

What Is Weather?

Fast Fact

About 25 centimeters (10 inches) of snow equals about 3 centimeters (1 inch) of rain. You can compare snow to other types of weather.

Daily Weather

You need

• paper

• markers

Observe the weather
each day for two weeks.

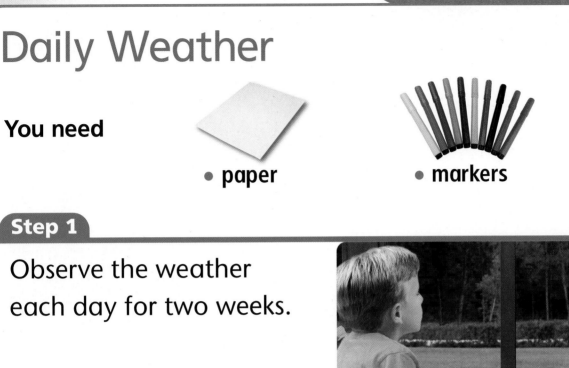

Make a chart. Record
what you see.

Daily Weather

Mon.	Tues.	Wed.	Thurs.	Fri.

Compare the weather
from day to day. Do
you see any patterns?
Predict next week's
weather.

Inquiry Skill

You can compare things
by telling how they are
alike and how they are
different.

VOCABULARY
weather

(Focus Skill) **READING FOCUS SKILL**

COMPARE AND CONTRAST Look for ways in which weather can be different from day to day.

Weather

Weather is what the air outside is like. You can see and feel the weather. It may be warm or cool. It may be snowy, windy, rainy, cloudy, or sunny.

What weather do you see here?

Weather can change. It may be sunny one day. The next day may be cloudy. It may be cold for many days. Then it may warm up. One day may be windy. Another day may be calm.

★ **COMPARE AND CONTRAST**
Focus Skill
How can weather be different from day to day?

Insta-Lab

Observing Weather

Look out the window. Observe the sky. Observe what people are wearing. What can you tell about the weather? Repeat each day for a week. Make a chart to show weather data.

Weather and You

You wear heavy clothes in cold weather. You wear light clothes in warm weather. When it rains, you wear clothes that help keep you dry. You may choose activities to go with the weather, too.

COMPARE AND CONTRAST **How is clothing for cold weather different from clothing for warm weather?**

What activities are these people doing?

228

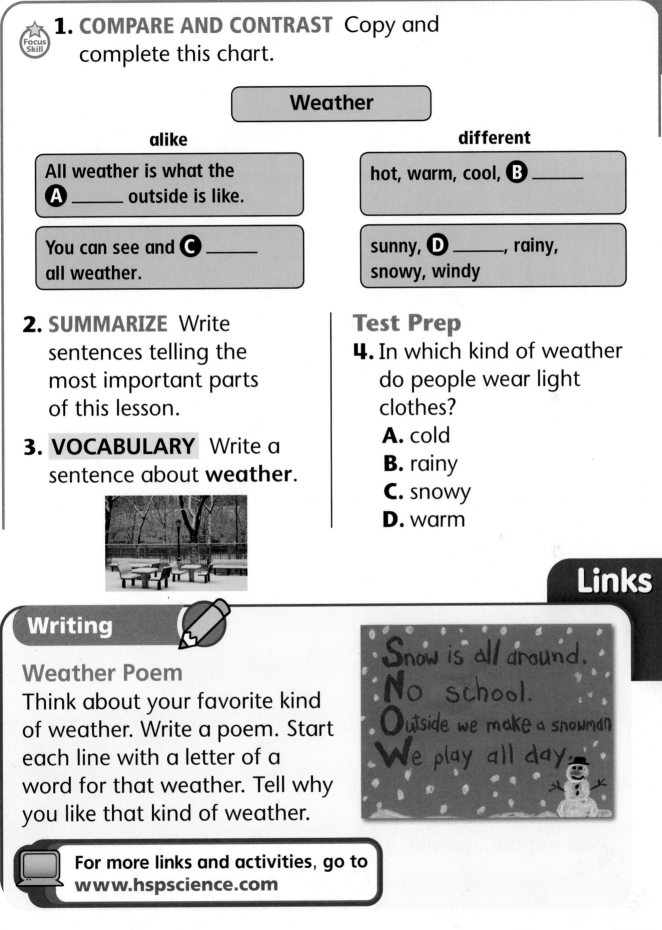

1. **COMPARE AND CONTRAST** Copy and complete this chart.

Weather

alike

All weather is what the **A** _____ outside is like.

You can see and **C** _____ all weather.

different

hot, warm, cool, **B** _____

sunny, **D** _____, rainy, snowy, windy

2. **SUMMARIZE** Write sentences telling the most important parts of this lesson.

3. **VOCABULARY** Write a sentence about **weather**.

Test Prep

4. In which kind of weather do people wear light clothes?
   A. cold
   B. rainy
   C. snowy
   D. warm

Links

Writing

Weather Poem
Think about your favorite kind of weather. Write a poem. Start each line with a letter of a word for that weather. Tell why you like that kind of weather.

Snow is all around.
No school.
Outside we make a snowman
We play all day.

For more links and activities, go to www.hspscience.com

229

How Can We Measure Weather?

Fast Fact

This tool shows the direction of the wind. How else do people measure weather?

Measure Temperature

You need

- **thermometer**
- **red crayon**

Step 1

Draw two thermometers. Label one **inside** and one **outside**.

Step 2

Measure the temperature inside and outside the classroom. Record on the thermometers you drew.

Step 3

How do your **measurements** help you know where it is warmer?

Inquiry Skill

When you **measure** with a thermometer, you find out the temperature.

READING FOCUS SKILL

MAIN IDEA AND DETAILS Look for the main ideas about measuring weather.

Measuring Temperature

One way to measure weather is to find the temperature. **Temperature** is the measure of how hot or cold something is. A **thermometer** is a tool for measuring temperature.

thermometer

MAIN IDEA AND DETAILS How can you find out how warm the air is outside?

Measuring Rain

You can also measure how much rain falls. This tool is a rain gauge. It shows how much rain has fallen.

⭐ **MAIN IDEA AND DETAILS**
How can you measure rain?

rain gauge

Insta-Lab

Where's the Heat?
Find the warmest place in your classroom. Use a thermometer. Measure the temperature in different places. Tell what you find out.

233

Measuring Wind

You can measure wind, too. An anemometer measures the speed of the wind. A weather vane shows the direction of the wind. A windsock also shows the direction of the wind.

⭐ **Focus Skill** **MAIN IDEA AND DETAILS**

What are two tools that measure the direction of wind?

weather vane

anemometer

windsocks

1. MAIN IDEA AND DETAILS Copy and complete this chart.

> ## Measuring Weather

> ### Main Idea
> You can measure weather in many ways.

| **detail** You can measure **A** _____, which is how hot or cold it is. | **detail** You can measure how much **B** _____ has fallen. | **detail** You can measure the **C** _____ and **D** _____ of the wind. |

2. DRAW CONCLUSIONS
How can measuring weather help people?

3. VOCABULARY
Use the words **temperature** and **thermometer** to tell about the picture.

Test Prep
4. What are three ways you can measure weather?

Links

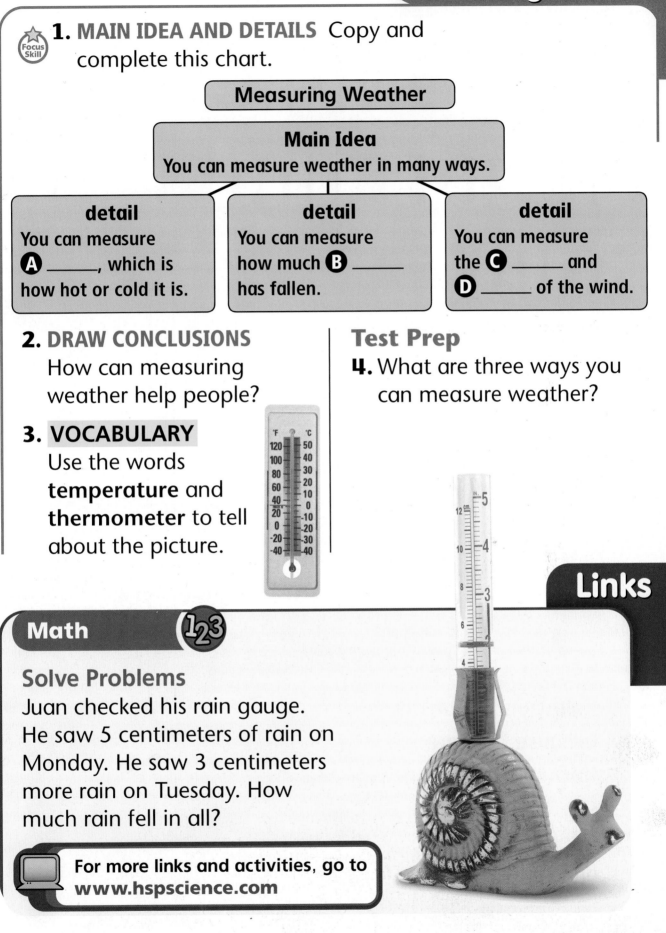

Math

Solve Problems
Juan checked his rain gauge. He saw 5 centimeters of rain on Monday. He saw 3 centimeters more rain on Tuesday. How much rain fell in all?

> **For more links and activities, go to www.hspscience.com**

What Makes Clouds and Rain?

Fast Fact

Rain clouds look dark because they are thick and block the sun. What can you infer about rain and clouds?

Make Clouds

You need

- jar with lid
- hot water
- ice cubes

Step 1

Let your teacher put the hot water in the jar. Wait one minute. Then pour most of it out. **CAUTION:** hot water!

Step 2

Turn the jar lid upside down. Place it on the jar. Observe.

Step 3

Place ice on the lid. Observe. **Infer** how clouds form.

Inquiry Skill

To **infer** what happens, observe carefully. Then draw a conclusion.

237

(Focus Skill) **READING FOCUS SKILL**

CAUSE AND EFFECT Look for what causes clouds and rain to form.

The Water Cycle

Clouds and rain are part of the water cycle. In the **water cycle**, water moves from Earth to the air and back again.

Science Up Close

The Water Cycle

1 The sun makes water warm. This causes the water to **evaporate**, or change to water vapor. **Water vapor** is water in the air that you can not see.

2 Water vapor meets cool air. The cool air causes the water vapor to **condense**, or change into tiny water drops. The drops form clouds.

3 Water drops come together and get bigger and heavier. Then they fall as rain or snow.

4 Some rain and snow falls into rivers, lakes, and oceans. Some flows there from the land.

5 The cycle continues.

For more links and activities, go to www.hspscience.com

239

Clouds

Clouds are clues about how the weather may change.

 CAUSE AND EFFECT What kind of clouds bring rain or snow?

Insta-Lab

Cloud Journal

Keep a journal of clouds and the weather. Each morning, draw the clouds you see. Predict what the weather will be like. Later, check to see if your predictions were right.

Clouds	Weather
cumulus	Some clouds look like puffy white cotton. They often mean nice weather.
stratus	Other clouds are gray, flat, and low in the sky. They may bring rain or snow.
cirrus	These clouds look like thin, white feathers. They often mean sunny weather.

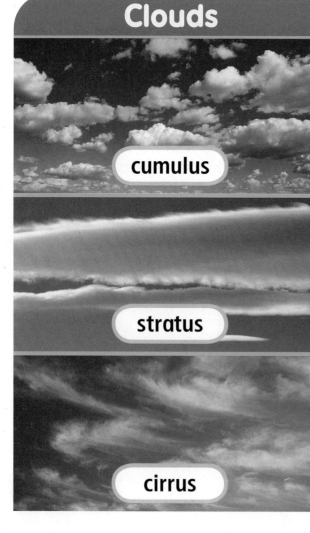

240

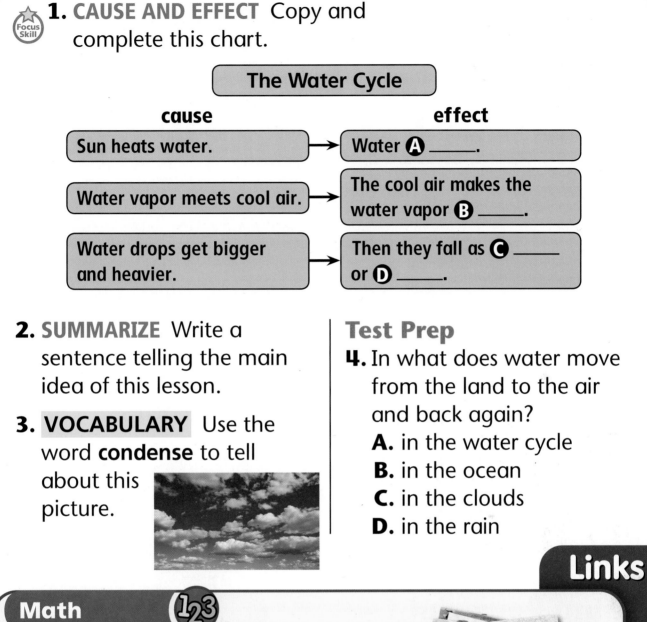

1. CAUSE AND EFFECT Copy and complete this chart.

The Water Cycle

cause		effect
Sun heats water.	→	Water **Ⓐ** _____.
Water vapor meets cool air.	→	The cool air makes the water vapor **Ⓑ** _____.
Water drops get bigger and heavier.	→	Then they fall as **Ⓒ** _____ or **Ⓓ** _____.

2. SUMMARIZE Write a sentence telling the main idea of this lesson.

3. VOCABULARY Use the word **condense** to tell about this picture.

Test Prep

4. In what does water move from the land to the air and back again?

A. in the water cycle
B. in the ocean
C. in the clouds
D. in the rain

Links

Math

Use Ordinal Numbers

Work with a partner to draw the steps of the water cycle. Write about each step. First, the sun heats the water. Use second, third, and fourth to retell the other steps.

For more links and activities, go to www.hspscience.com

First, the sun heats the water.

Is the Weather Getting Worse?

Earth's weather can get pretty wild. Scientists say that Earth's weather is getting wilder. That's because Earth's temperature is rising.

Using Powerful Tools

Weather experts use satellites to study weather. Satellites with cameras are launched into space. The satellites take pictures showing Earth's weather.

The pictures are sent to weather experts. The experts then use computers. The computers help predict what the weather will be in the future.

Looking Back

Weather experts looked at weather in the past. They compared that weather with today's weather. The experts say the study showed that the world's weather is changing.

Scientists say the change is because Earth's temperature is rising. This change might mean less rain will fall in the future. Or, it may mean that summer weather will last longer.

Warming Warning!

Scientists say that the world's weather will keep getting worse if the warming does not stop.

THINK ABOUT IT

How do satellites help weather experts?

Find out more! Log on to **www.hspscience.com**

Watching the Weather

Bob Stokes is a special kind of scientist. He studies the weather. He can tell when the weather will change.

Stokes can also tell when a thunderstorm might happen. Thunderstorms can bring strong winds and heavy rain. They can harm people and their homes. If people know what kind of weather is coming, they can try to be safe. Stokes is helping people do that.

You Can Do It!

Explore Evaporation

What to Do

1. Put the same amount of water in each cup. Put a piece of tape on each cup to mark the waterline. Cover one cup tightly with plastic wrap.
2. Put both cups in a warm place.
3. Wait one day. Compare the water in the cups. Talk about what you see.

Materials
- 2 plastic cups
- water
- tape
- plastic wrap

Draw Conclusions
What happened to the water in each cup? Why do you think that happened?

Weather Safety

Make a poster about weather safety. Show ways you stay safe in different kinds of weather. Tell ways to stay safe in the sun, in snowstorms, and in rainstorms. Share your poster with the class.

Weather Safety

Wear sunscreen. Stay cool.

Wear warm clothes.

Wear a raincoat. Go inside if the rain is heavy.

Review and Test Preparation

Vocabulary Review

Use the words below to complete the sentences.

weather p. 226   **evaporate** p. 238

thermometer p. 232   **water vapor** p. 238

1. A tool that measures temperature is a ____.

2. Warmth may cause water to ____.

3. Water in the air is ____.

4. The air outside is ____.

Check Understanding

5. What is the **cause** for each **effect** labeled with an arrow in the water cycle?

6. Which tool would you use to find out how fast the wind is blowing?

A. anemometer

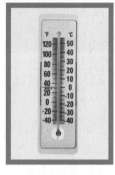

C. thermometer

B. rain gauge

D. weather vane

7. What do clouds give clues about?

F. temperature

G. how windy it is

H. how much it will rain

J. what the weather will be

Critical Thinking

8. You are getting dressed for school. How can you make sure you wear the right clothes for the weather?

Vocabulary

season

spring

summer

fall

migrate

winter

I wonder...

Why do some leaves change color?

What do **you** wonder?

249

What Is Spring?

Fast Fact

Early spring is the best time to plant a vegetable garden. You can hypothesize about what helps plants grow in spring.

Plants and Light

You need

- **young plant**
- **shoe box with hole**
- **spray bottle**

Step 1

Put the plant in the box.
Put the lid on the box.

Step 2

Place the box so that
the hole faces a window.
Hypothesize about what
will happen to the plant.

Step 3

Spray the plant with
water each day.
After one week, what
happens? Was your
hypothesis correct?

Inquiry Skill

When you **hypothesize**,
you think of an idea.

251

READING FOCUS SKILL

MAIN IDEA AND DETAILS Look for the main ideas about spring.

Seasons

A **season** is a time of year. A year has four seasons. The seasons are spring, summer, fall, and winter. They form a pattern. After every winter comes spring.

Science Up Close

Seasons

March

Sunday	Monday	Tuesday	Wednesday	Thursday	Friday	Saturday
		2	3	4	5	6
1						
8	9	10	11	12	13	
14	15	16	17	18	19	20
21	22	23	24	25	26	27
28	29	30	31			

Spring starts in the month of March.

252

spring

summer

fall

winter

253

Spring

Spring is the season after winter. In spring, the weather gets warmer. There may be many rainy days. Spring has more hours of daylight than winter. People may go outside more.

 MAIN IDEA AND DETAILS
What is the weather like in spring?

rain

How can you tell it is spring?

254

Plants in Spring

Many plants begin to grow in spring. They get more warmth, light, and rain in spring than in winter. Plants may grow new leaves and flowers.

★ Focus Skill MAIN IDEA AND DETAILS

Why do many plants grow well in spring?

flowers

flowering tree

255

Animals in Spring

Spring is a good time for many animals to have their young. New plants are food for the young. Some young animals are born. Others hatch from eggs. It is easy for them all to find food.

geese and goslings

 MAIN IDEA AND DETAILS
Why is spring a good time for animals to have their young?

ewe and lambs

1. **MAIN IDEA AND DETAILS** Copy and complete this chart.

Spring

Main Idea
Spring is one of the four seasons.

detail
The weather gets **A** _____ in spring.

detail
There are more hours of **B** _____.

detail
Many plants begin to **C** _____.

detail
Many animals have their **D** _____.

2. **SUMMARIZE** Use the chart to write a lesson summary.

3. **VOCABULARY** Tell about the **season** in this picture.

Test Prep

4. What helps plants grow in spring?
   A. freezing
   B. seasons
   C. warmth, light, and rain
   D. young animals

Links

Writing

Spring Stories
Write a story about a young animal in spring. Tell about what the animal sees and does. Use what you know about animals in spring to write your story.

For more links and activities, go to www.hspscience.com

The bunny was born. It ate lots of plants. It hopped in the grass.

What Is Summer?

Fast Fact

There are more kinds of shells than you can count. Many people collect shells in summer. You can infer why people do different activities in different seasons.

258

Hot Weather Activities

You need

● **seasons picture cards**

Step 1

Work with a partner. Talk about what people do in summer.

Step 2

Look at each card. Find clues that tell about the season. **Infer** which pictures show summer.

Step 3

Compare your ideas with other classmates' ideas. How do you know which pictures show summer?

Inquiry Skill

To **infer**, you use what you already know to figure out something.

Reading in Science

(Focus Skill) **READING FOCUS SKILL**

MAIN IDEA AND DETAILS Look for the main ideas about summer.

Summer

Summer is the season after spring. Like spring, it has many hours of daylight. Summer weather can be hot. People wear light clothes. Some places may have thunderstorms.

 MAIN IDEA AND DETAILS
What is summer?

hot weather

How can you tell it is summer?

Plants in Summer

Summer weather helps many plants grow. Trees have many green leaves. Some plants grow fruits.

★ MAIN IDEA AND DETAILS
How can plants change in summer?

Insta-Lab

Act Out Summer Activities

Think about things you like to do in summer. Act them out. Ask others to guess what they are. Why is summer a good time to do each thing?

tomato plant

tree with leaves

Animals in Summer

In summer, animals have ways to stay cool. Some cool off in mud or water. Others lose fur so that their coats are lighter.

Young animals can find plants and other food. They grow bigger.

pig cooling off in mud

★ MAIN IDEA AND DETAILS

What is one way animals stay cool in summer?

bison shedding fur

Focus Skill

1. MAIN IDEA AND DETAILS Copy and complete this chart.

Summer

Main Idea
Summer is the season after spring.

detail
The weather can be **A** _____.

detail
Some plants grow **B** _____.

detail
Animals have ways to stay **C** _____.

2. DRAW CONCLUSIONS Why do some people like cold drinks in summer?

3. VOCABULARY Use the word **summer** to tell about the picture.

Test Prep

4. Write about how plants change from spring to summer.

Links

Math 123

Use a Calendar
Use a calendar to answer these questions. How many months are there? What are their names? Which ones are summer months? When does summer begin? When does it end?

For more links and activities, go to **www.hspscience.com**

			JUNE			
SUN	MON	TUE	WED	THU	FRI	SAT
			1	2	3	4
5	6	7	8	9	10	11
12	13	14	15	16	17	18
19	20	21	22	23	24	25
26	27	28	29	30		

What Is Fall?

Fast Fact

Apples get ripe in fall.
People pick the apples
and make them into
foods to eat all year.
You can compare
fruits in many ways.

Compare Seeds

You need

- **fruits with seeds**
- **hand lens**

Step 1

Look at the fruits with the hand lens. Find the seeds. **Compare** the seeds. How are they alike? How are they different?

Step 2

Draw and label pictures of the fruits and seeds.

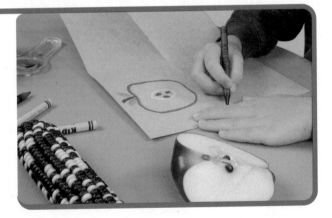

Step 3

Talk about how the seeds are alike. Then talk about how they are different.

Inquiry Skill

Look at the sizes, shapes, and colors of the seeds to **compare** them.

(Focus Skill) **READING FOCUS SKILL**

CAUSE AND EFFECT Look for reasons that plants and animals change in fall.

Fall

Fall is the season after summer. It has fewer hours of daylight than summer. The temperature gets cooler. People wear heavier clothes.

(Focus Skill) **CAUSE AND EFFECT** Why do people wear heavier clothes in fall?

How can you tell it is fall?

cleaning up leaves

266

Plants in Fall

In many places, leaves change color and fall from the trees. This happens because they do not get as much daylight as in summer.

Some fruits get ripe in fall. Then they are ready to pick and eat.

CAUSE AND EFFECT Why do we pick some fruits in fall?

Insta-Lab

Swim!

Why do you swim in summer and not in fall? Put a cup of water under a lamp. **CAUTION:** The lamp may be hot! Put another cup of water in a shady place. Which cup of water warms up faster?

squashes

maple trees

Animals in Fall

As the air gets cooler, food may be harder for animals to find. Some animals store food to eat later. Others **migrate**, or move to new places, to find food.

squirrel carrying food

 CAUSE AND EFFECT
Why do some animals store food in fall?

geese migrating

Focus Skill

1. CAUSE AND EFFECT Copy and complete this chart.

Fall

cause		effect
Weather gets **A** _____ in fall.	→	People wear **B** _____ clothes.
There is not as much **C** _____.	→	Some trees lose their **D** _____.
There is not as much food for **E** _____.	→	Some animals **F** _____ food for later.

2. SUMMARIZE Use the chart to summarize what happens in fall.

3. VOCABULARY Use the word **fall** to tell about these plants.

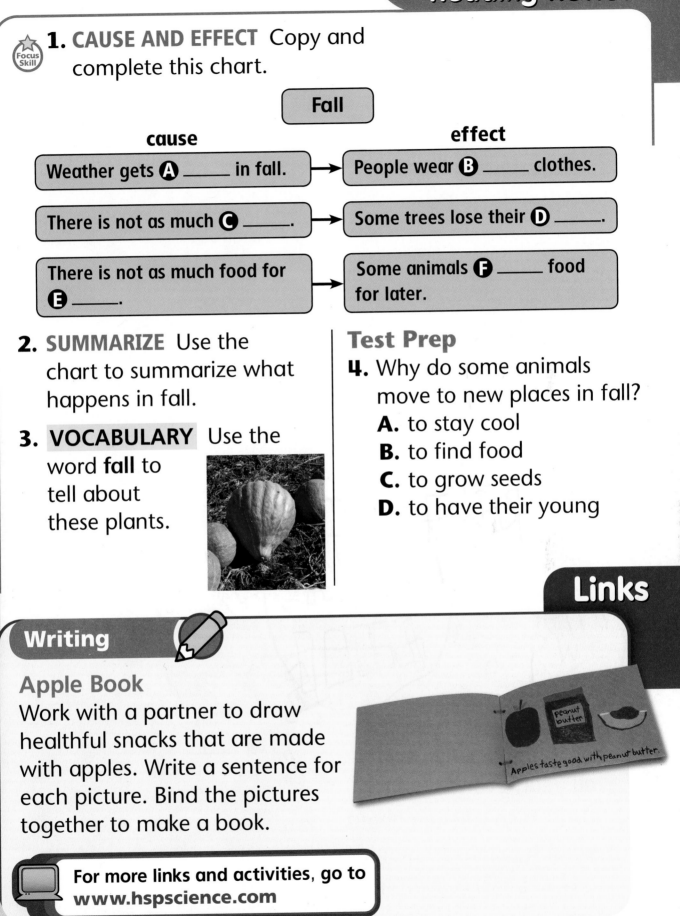

Test Prep

4. Why do some animals move to new places in fall?

  A. to stay cool
  B. to find food
  C. to grow seeds
  D. to have their young

Links

Writing

Apple Book

Work with a partner to draw healthful snacks that are made with apples. Write a sentence for each picture. Bind the pictures together to make a book.

For more links and activities, go to www.hspscience.com

peanut butter

Apples taste good with peanut butter.

What Is Winter?

Fast Fact

Some trees stay green all year, even in winter. Draw a conclusion about what happens to plants and animals in winter.

How to Stay Warm

You need

• plastic bag

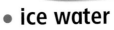

• ice water

• mitten

Step 1

Put your hand in the bag. Dip the bag into the water. How does your hand feel?

Step 2

Put on the mitten. Put your hand in the bag, and dip the bag into the water. How does your hand feel?

Step 3

Draw a conclusion about what can keep you warm in winter.

Inquiry Skill

To draw a conclusion, use what you observed to decide what something means.

271

Reading in Science

Winter

Winter is the season after fall. Winter has fewer hours of daylight. In some places, the air is cold. Snow may fall. People in these places wear very heavy clothes. In other places, the air may just get cooler.

How can you tell it is winter?

Focus Skill **MAIN IDEA AND DETAILS** How is winter different from fall?

272

Plants in Winter

Many plants have no leaves in winter. Other plants stay green.

Some plants rest. They do not grow until it gets warm again. Other plants die.

 MAIN IDEA AND DETAILS
What can happen to plants in the winter?

Insta-Lab

Cold-Weather Clothes
Draw a picture of yourself in very cold weather. Label each thing you wear to stay warm. Then show your work to a partner. Tell how each piece of clothing keeps you warm.

holly

bare tree

273

Animals in Winter

Food can be hard to find in winter. Some animals eat food that they stored in fall. Others sleep until spring.

Some animals change color to stay safe. Some grow thick coats to stay warm.

⭐ **MAIN IDEA AND DETAILS** How do some animals change in winter?

This animal changes color in winter.

This animal grows a thick coat in winter.

Focus Skill

1. MAIN IDEA AND DETAILS Copy and complete this chart.

Winter

Main Idea
Winter is the season after fall.

| **detail** The weather may get **A** _____. | **detail** In some places, **B** _____ falls. | **detail** Plants may rest or **C** _____. | **detail** Some animals grow thick **D** _____ to stay warm. |

2. DRAW CONCLUSIONS Why do you think it is hard for animals to find food in winter?

3. VOCABULARY Tell how you know this picture shows winter.

Test Prep

4. How can winter be different in different places?

Links

Social Studies

Snowy Places
Look at a map of the United States. Find places in the United States where it snows in winter. Where are these places? Make a list. Tell how the places are alike.

It snows in
1. New York
2. Maine
3. Montana

For more links and activities, go to www.hspscience.com

Snow Is Useful

When snow falls, it is soft and fluffy. Over time, it gets packed down.

Snow is strong and holds heat well. Some people use it to build homes. These homes are called igloos.

The Inuit

Canada is a country north of the United States. In Canada, there is a group of people called Inuit. Sometimes the Inuit have to travel during the winter. They move across large areas of snow and ice.

To use a tent on the snow and ice would be too cold. So the Inuit use snow to build an igloo.

The Inuit cut snow into blocks. Then they stack the blocks into a curved shape. It looks sort of like the top of your head. A narrow tunnel is built. It is used to get into the igloo. The tunnel stops the wind from blowing in.

- The largest snowflake was almost a foot across.
- No two snowflakes are alike.
- All snowflakes have six sides.
- Stampede Pass, Washington, is the snow capital of the United States!

THINK ABOUT IT

Why do you think igloos are built only during the winter?

Find out more! Log on to **www.hspscience.com**

Meet Ivy the Inventor

During the fall and winter, it gets dark outside earlier. That means things like mailboxes may be hard to see. Ivy Lumpkin came up with an idea to help people see mailboxes better.

Ivy put two nightlights into a clear tube. The lights run on batteries. Then she put a mailbox on top of the tube. When it is dark out, the nightlights shine and people can see the post. Bright idea, Ivy!

Cool Colors

What to Do

1. Put a thermometer inside each T-shirt.

2. Put the T-shirts in a sunny place. Record the temperature in each.

3. Wait one hour. Record the temperatures. Which colors stayed cooler? Which color got the warmest?

Materials
- 3 thermometers
- 3 T-shirts

Draw Conclusions
What kinds of colors will help you stay cool?

Favorite Season Graphs

Take a survey. Find out which season your class likes best. Make a bar graph to show what you learn. Share your graph with your classmates.

Review and Test Preparation

Vocabulary Review

Match the word to its picture.

1. spring p. 254

3. fall p. 266

2. summer p. 260

4. winter p. 272

A.

C.

B.

D.

Check Understanding

5. What is a season? Tell **details** about one season.

6. In which season would you see trees with many green leaves? Tell why.

7. Why do some animals shed some of their fur in summer?

  A. to stay warm

  B. to hide

  C. to find food

  D. to stay cool

Critical Thinking

8. Tell how the tree changes with each season.

Objects in the Sky

Lesson 1 **What Can We See in the Sky?**

Lesson 2 **What Causes Day and Night?**

Lesson 3 **What Can We Observe About the Moon?**

Vocabulary

sun

star

moon

rotate

crater

I wonder...

Why can you sometimes see the moon in the daytime?

What do **YOU** wonder?

What Can We See in the Sky?

Fast Fact

Moving air causes some of the light from the stars to bend. This makes the stars seem to twinkle. You can communicate about what you see in the sky.

The Daytime Sky

You need

- colored paper
- crayons

Step 1

Look out the window.
Observe the daytime sky.

Step 2

Draw pictures of what
you see. Write about it.

Step 3

Share your work with a
partner. Use it to help
you **communicate** what
you observed.

Inquiry Skill

You can use writing and
pictures to help you
communicate.

VOCABULARY

sun
star
moon

Focus Skill **READING FOCUS SKILL**

COMPARE AND CONTRAST Look for ways the daytime and nighttime skies are alike and ways they are different.

Observing the Sky

In the daytime sky, you may see clouds and the sun. The **sun** is the star closest to Earth. A **star** is an object in the sky that gives off its own light. The sun lights Earth in the daytime.

sun

clouds

In the nighttime sky, you may see stars, planets, and the moon. The **moon** is a huge ball of rock. It does not give off its own light. Its light comes from the sun.

moon

★ Focus Skill COMPARE AND CONTRAST How are the daytime sky and the nighttime sky different?

planet

stars

Insta-Lab

Moonlight

Cover a ball with foil. Have a partner shine a flashlight at the ball. Does the ball seem brighter when it is lit up? How is the ball like the moon? How is the flashlight like the sun?

Telescopes

You can look at the sky with a telescope. A telescope is a tool that makes things that are far away look closer. It can help you see more of the moon, stars, and planets.

Look at the planet Mars with just your eyes. This is what you see.

Look at Mars with a telescope. This is what you see. How much more can you see now?

For more links and activities, go to www.hspscience.com

288

1. COMPARE AND CONTRAST Copy and complete this chart.

alike	different
In the daytime and nighttime sky, you can sometimes see clouds and the moon.	In the daytime sky, you may see **A** _____ and the sun.
	In the nighttime sky, you may see **B** _____, planets, and the moon.
	In the daytime, the **C** _____ gives off light.
	In the nighttime, the stars give off light, but the **D** _____ does not.

2. DRAW CONCLUSIONS Why do you think the sun is much brighter than the moon?

3. VOCABULARY Use the words **sun** and **star** to talk about this picture.

Test Prep

4. What does a telescope do?

  A. It makes things that are far away look closer.

  B. It makes things that are close look farther away.

  C. It makes very big things look farther away.

  D. It makes very big things look smaller.

Links

Writing

Stories About the Sky

Long ago, people made up stories about what they saw in the sky. Write your own story about something in the sky. Then draw a picture for your story.

The sun is a happy teacher. The clouds are her students.

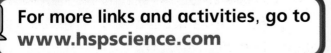

For more links and activities, go to **www.hspscience.com**

What Causes Day and Night?

Fast Fact

When it is daytime in the United States, it is nighttime in China. You can make a model to see why this happens.

Model Day and Night

You need

- labels
- tape
- globe
- flashlight

Step 1

Label the globe Earth.
Label the flashlight sun.
Use them to **make a model**
of Earth and the sun.

Step 2

Make the room dark. Have
a partner hold the globe.
Shine the flashlight on it.

Step 3

How does the **model**
help you see why Earth
has day and night?

Inquiry Skill

Make a model to help
you see why something
happens.

READING FOCUS SKILL

CAUSE AND EFFECT Look for what causes day and night.

Day and Night

Each day, the sun seems to move across the sky. It is not the sun that is moving. It is Earth! Earth rotates. To **rotate** is to spin like a top.

United States

SCHOOL BUS

STOP

day

As Earth rotates, the side we live on turns toward the sun. The sun lights the sky, and we have day. As Earth keeps rotating, our side turns away from the sun. The sky gets dark, and we have night.

CAUSE AND EFFECT **What do we have when the side of Earth we live on turns toward the sun? Why?**

United States

night

Objects in the Sky Seem to Move

The sun, moon, and stars seem to move in the sky. As Earth spins, we turn toward and away from the sun, moon, and stars. We can not feel that we are moving, so it seems to us as if they are.

★ **CAUSE AND EFFECT** Why does the sun seem to move in the sky?

Things Seem to Move

Stand in an open space. Turn around in circles. Do the things around you seem to move? How is this like the way the sun and stars seem to move around Earth?

noon

morning

evening

Focus Skill

1. CAUSE AND EFFECT Copy and complete this chart.

Day and Night

cause

As Earth **A** _____, the side we live on turns toward the sun.

effect

The **B** _____ lights the sky, and we have **C** _____.

→

The side we live on turns away from the **D** _____.

We have **E** _____.

→

2. SUMMARIZE Use the chart to write a summary of the lesson.

3. VOCABULARY Use the word **rotate** to talk about this picture.

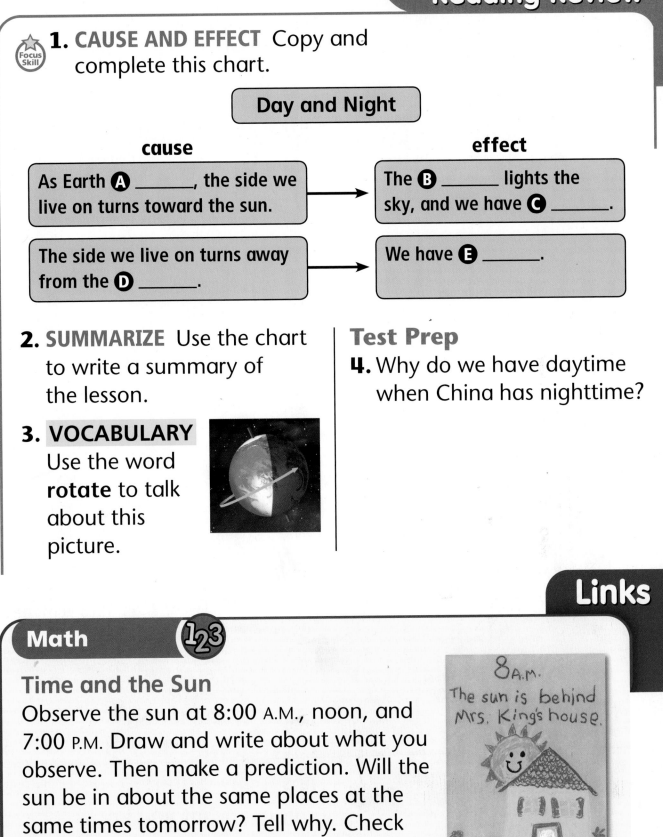

Test Prep

4. Why do we have daytime when China has nighttime?

Links

Math 123

Time and the Sun

Observe the sun at 8:00 A.M., noon, and 7:00 P.M. Draw and write about what you observe. Then make a prediction. Will the sun be in about the same places at the same times tomorrow? Tell why. Check tomorrow to see if you were right.

8 A.M.
The sun is behind Mrs. King's house.

For more links and activities, go to **www.hspscience.com**

What Can We Observe About the Moon?

Fast Fact

Much of the moon is covered with dust. It has many craters. You can use what you know to infer how the craters were made.

The Surface of the Moon

You need

- **pan of sand**

- **spray bottle of water**

- **marbles**

Step 1

Spray the sand lightly with water.

Step 2

Hold the marbles above the sand. Drop them one at a time. Observe.

Step 3

Infer how the moon's craters were made. Compare your ideas with others' ideas.

Inquiry Skill

To **infer**, first observe. Then think about what you see.

VOCABULARY
crater

(Focus Skill) **READING FOCUS SKILL**

SEQUENCE Look for the order in which the moon seems to change.

Changes in the Moon's Shape

The shape of the moon seems to change a little each night. The changes make a pattern that takes about 29 days.

On some nights, you can not see the moon at all. Then you start to see a little of it. After about 15 days, you see the moon as a full circle. Then you see less of it each night. In about 14 more days, you can not see it again.

Day 22
quarter moon

(Focus Skill) **SEQUENCE** What happens to the moon after you see it as a full circle?

Insta-Lab

Moon Changes

The picture cards show how the moon looks. Put them in order. Start with the new moon. Then use the pictures to tell about how the moon seems to change.

**Day 1
new moon**

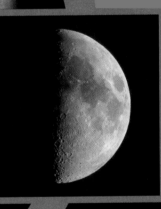

**Day 8
quarter moon**

**Day 15
full moon**

Exploring the Moon

In 1969, astronauts landed on the moon for the first time. First, they saw the moon's gray dust and craters. A **crater** is a hole that is shaped like a bowl in a surface. Next, the astronauts explored the moon. Later, they brought moon rocks back to Earth.

SEQUENCE What did the astronauts do after they landed on the moon?

astronaut on the moon

footprints in moon dust

moon rock

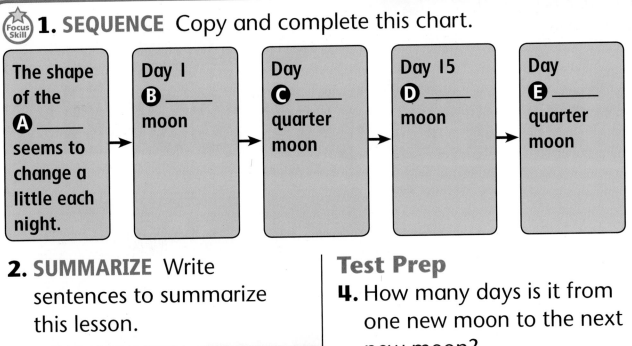

Focus Skill **1. SEQUENCE** Copy and complete this chart.

| The shape of the **A** _____ seems to change a little each night. | → | Day 1 **B** _____ moon | → | Day **C** _____ quarter moon | → | Day 15 **D** _____ moon | → | Day **E** _____ quarter moon |

2. SUMMARIZE Write sentences to summarize this lesson.

3. VOCABULARY Use the word **crater** to talk about this picture.

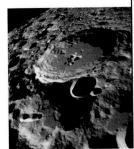

Test Prep

4. How many days is it from one new moon to the next new moon?

A. 8
B. 15
C. 22
D. 29

Writing

Writing About the Moon

Research what the moon is like. Then write sentences about exploring the moon yourself. What would you do there? What would you want to find out? Draw pictures to go with your sentences.

I would walk in the craters.

For more links and activities, go to **www.hspscience.com**

Smart Spacesuits

Right now, people are living and working on the space station. The people are called astronauts.

Spacesuits have to protect astronauts from the cold. The suits also have to let astronauts move their arms and hands. That is so the astronauts can add parts or do repairs.

Breathtaking Fact

When astronauts go outside, they wear special spacesuits. That is because it is very cold in space and there is no air to breathe.

Scientists have made the spacesuits better. They added a computer that is sewn into the suit. The computer will help astronauts do their work.

Scientists also made the gloves better. Now, the fingers and thumbs are much easier to move. The gloves are also heated to help the astronauts work outside longer.

THINK ABOUT IT

Why do you think astronauts have to wear special suits?

Find out more! Log on to
www.hspscience.com

Studying Mars

Joy Crisp loves rocks and volcanoes. Now she is studying rocks and volcanoes on Mars. Mars is a planet in space.

Crisp uses machines on Earth to watch two robot rovers on Mars. The rovers are like little radio controlled trucks. They use special tools to study rocks and dirt.

Scientists are looking to find if Mars ever had water. If so, scientists say people might someday live on Mars.

You Can Do It!

Warm or Cool

Materials
- thermometer

What to Do

1. When is it warmest outside? Make a chart. Predict what you will find out.

2. Use a thermometer. Find the temperature at three different times of day.

3. Write the temperatures in the chart. Were your predictions correct?

Draw Conclusions

Why is the temperature different at different times of day? What does the sun do to Earth?

Moon Journal

Keep a moon journal. Go outside with a family member each night for one month. Find the moon. Draw what you observe. Write the date on each picture. After one month, bind your drawings into a book. Share it with the class.

Review and Test Preparation

Vocabulary Review

Choose the best word to complete each sentence.

sun p. 286	rotate p. 292
moon p. 287	crater p. 300

1. A word that means spin is ___.

2. A ball of rock whose light comes from the sun is the ___.

3. The star closest to Earth is the ___.

4. A hole in the surface of the moon that is shaped like a bowl is a ___.

Check Understanding

5. Explain the **effect** when our side of Earth turns toward the sun. Use this picture to help you.

6. Which object in the sky gives off its own light?

   A. cloud   **C.** moon

   B. Earth   **D.** star

7. Each photo is part of a **sequence**. Which one shows the moon eight days after a new moon?

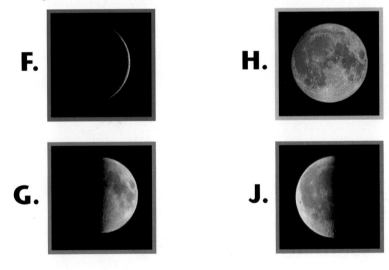

   F.   **H.**

   G.   **J.**

Critical Thinking

8. Juan looks at the sky and sees what this picture shows. Tell what you know about each object he sees.

Investigating Matter

Chapter 10 All About Matter

Albuquerque International Balloon Fiesta

TO: carmen@hspscience.com
FROM: louisa@hspscience.com
RE: Albuquerque, New Mexico

Dear Carmen,

Marta and I went to a festival. Lots of colored balloons floated in the sky. People took rides in the baskets. I got to ride in one too!

Louisa

Louisiana Children's Museum

TO: ed@hspscience.com

FROM: erica@hspscience.com

RE: New Orleans, Louisiana

Dear Ed,

My aunt and I went to the science museum. I was in a bubble that was bigger than me! We had so much fun.

Erica

Experiment!

Water Solutions As you do this unit, you will find out about things around you. Plan and do a test. Find out what happens to salt when it is mixed with warm or cold water.

309

10 All About Matter

Vocabulary

matter	dissolve
solid	float
mixture	sink
length	gas
mass	steam
liquid	

I wonder...

Why do things filled with air float in water?

What do **you** wonder?

What Is Matter?

Fast Fact

The largest stuffed
bear was 32 feet
tall. You can classify
toys by size, shape,
and color.

Classify Matter

You need

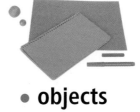

- **objects**

Step 1

Observe the objects. Compare their sizes, shapes, and colors.

Step 2

Classify the objects in three ways.

Step 3

Draw pictures of the groups you made.

Inquiry Skill

When you **classify** objects, you sort them by how they are alike.

VOCABULARY
matter

(Focus Skill) **READING FOCUS SKILL**

COMPARE AND CONTRAST Look for ways matter can be alike and different.

Matter

Everything around you is **matter**. Toys are matter. Balloons are matter. Water is matter, too. Some matter has parts that are too hard to see.

What matter do you see here?

All matter is not the same. Matter can be soft or hard. It can be big or small.

COMPARE AND CONTRAST
How are the stuffed toy and balloons alike? How are they different?

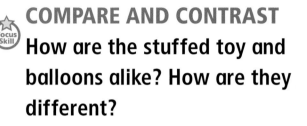

Insta-Lab

Matter Up Close

Observe sand and soil with a hand lens. How are they alike? How are they different? What does the hand lens help you see? Talk to a partner about what you see.

Sorting Matter

You can sort matter. You can sort these objects by color. You can sort them by shape. How else can you sort them?

 COMPARE AND CONTRAST
How could you sort these objects by color?

Focus Skill

1. COMPARE AND CONTRAST Copy and complete this chart.

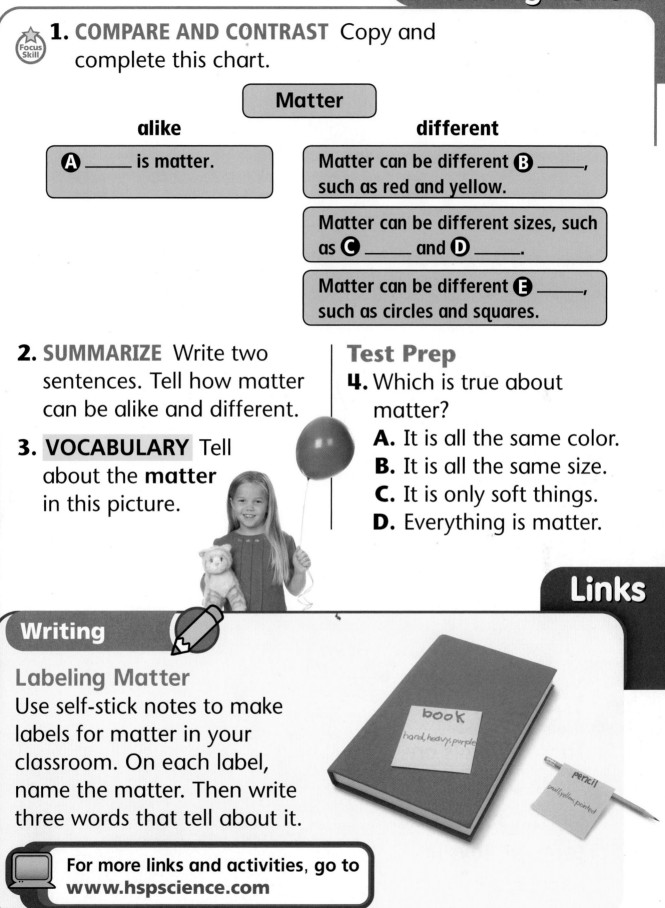

Matter

alike

A _____ is matter.

different

Matter can be different **B** _____, such as red and yellow.

Matter can be different sizes, such as **C** _____ and **D** _____.

Matter can be different **E** _____, such as circles and squares.

2. SUMMARIZE Write two sentences. Tell how matter can be alike and different.

3. VOCABULARY Tell about the **matter** in this picture.

Test Prep

4. Which is true about matter?
   A. It is all the same color.
   B. It is all the same size.
   C. It is only soft things.
   D. Everything is matter.

Links

Writing

Labeling Matter
Use self-stick notes to make labels for matter in your classroom. On each label, name the matter. Then write three words that tell about it.

book
hard, heavy, purple

pencil
small, yellow, pointed

For more links and activities, go to www.hspscience.com

What Can We Observe About Solids?

Fast Fact

These animals are made of millions of toy blocks. You can compare toys in many ways.

Measuring Mass

You need

- **2 blocks**

- **balance**

Step 1

Put a block on each side of the balance.

Step 2

Look at the blocks on the balance. **Compare**.

Step 3

Which block has more mass? Which has less mass?

Inquiry Skill

When you compare with a balance, you see how much mass things have.

319

VOCABULARY

solid
mixture
length
mass

READING FOCUS SKILL

MAIN IDEA AND DETAILS Look for the main ideas about solids.

Observing Solids

How are paper, scissors, and a globe the same? They are all solids.

A **solid** is a kind of matter that keeps its shape. It keeps its shape even when you move it.

MAIN IDEA AND DETAILS
How do you know musical instruments are solids?

Mixing Solids

When you mix different kinds of matter together, you make a **mixture**. A mixture is made up of two or more things. These drawing tools make a mixture of solids.

The things in a mixture do not change. You can sort them back out of the mixture.

★ Focus Skill
MAIN IDEA AND DETAILS
What is a mixture made up of?

This boy sorts the tools in the mixture.

Insta-Lab

Make Mixtures
Get small things from the classroom. Mix them together. Then trade mixtures with a partner. Sort the things back out of each other's mixtures.

Measuring Solids

You can measure solids. You can measure how long a solid is. That is its **length**. You measure length with a ruler.

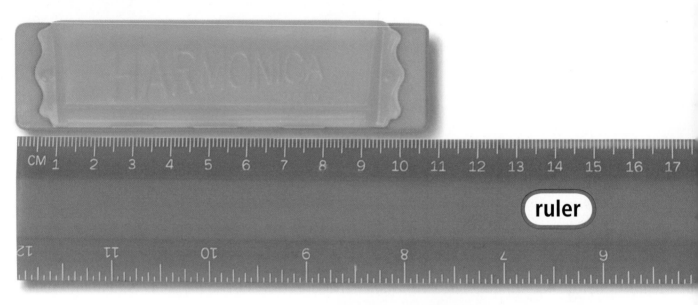

ruler

You can measure the mass of a solid. **Mass** is the amount of matter a solid has. You measure mass with a balance.

MAIN IDEA AND DETAILS What are two ways you can measure solids?

balance

Focus Skill

1. MAIN IDEA AND DETAILS Copy and complete this chart.

> **Solids**

> **Main Idea**
> A solid is matter that keeps its shape.

> **detail**
> You can mix solids.

> **detail**
> You can Ⓐ _____ solids.

2. DRAW CONCLUSIONS
How do you know a pencil is a solid?

3. VOCABULARY Tell about the **mass** of these blocks.

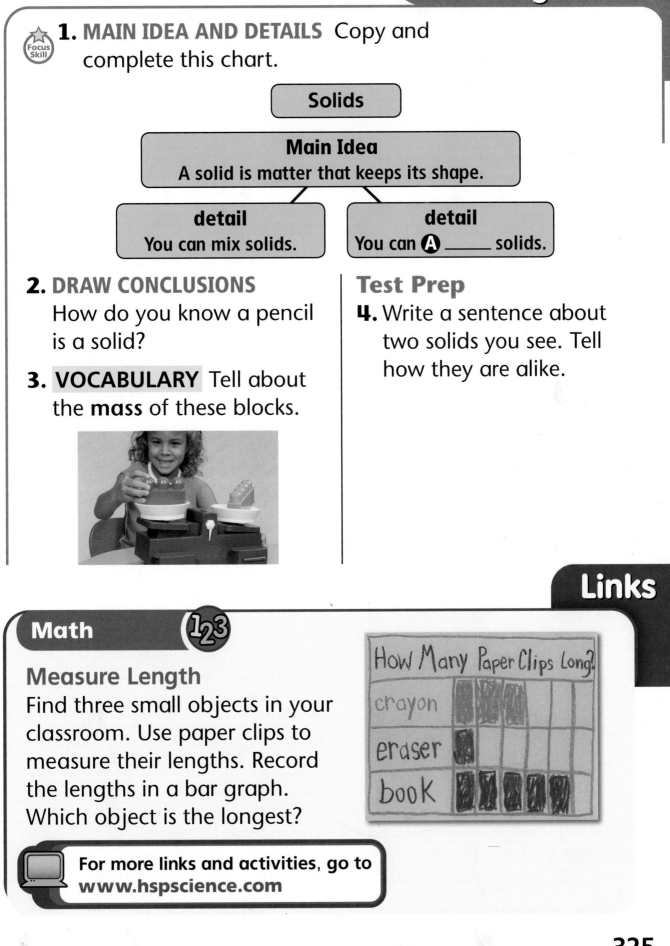

Test Prep

4. Write a sentence about two solids you see. Tell how they are alike.

Links

Math ①②③

Measure Length
Find three small objects in your classroom. Use paper clips to measure their lengths. Record the lengths in a bar graph. Which object is the longest?

How Many Paper Clips Long?
crayon				
eraser				
book				

For more links and activities, go to
www.hspscience.com

What Can We Observe About Liquids?

Fast Fact

Water is all around you. More than half of your body is water! You can measure water with tools.

The Shape of Liquids

You need

- **3 containers of water**
- **measuring cup**

Step 1

Look at the containers.
Draw their shapes.

Step 2

Predict which container
will have the most water.

Step 3

Measure the water in
each container. Was
your prediction right?

Inquiry Skill

When you measure
something, you use tools
to learn about it.

VOCABULARY
liquid
dissolve
float
sink

READING FOCUS SKILL

MAIN IDEA AND DETAILS Look for main ideas about liquids.

Observing Liquids

How are the soap and water alike? Both are liquids.

A **liquid** is matter that flows. It does not have its own shape. It takes the shape of its container.

MAIN IDEA AND DETAILS
What is a liquid?

liquid
soap

water

Liquid Mixtures

You can make mixtures with liquids. You can mix drink powder or salt with water. They **dissolve**, or mix completely with the liquid.

If you mix soil or oil with water, they do not dissolve.

MAIN IDEA AND DETAILS How can you tell if something dissolves?

Mix	Do Not Mix
juice	soil
salt	oil

Float and Sink

Does matter float or sink? You can test it.

Some objects **float**, or stay on top of a liquid.

Which objects sink?

Some objects **sink**, or fall to the bottom of a liquid.

⭐ **Focus Skill** **MAIN IDEA AND DETAILS** How can you find out if matter floats or sinks?

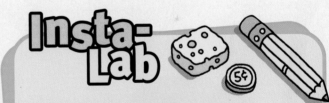

Insta-Lab

What Floats?

Get a coin, a pencil, and other classroom objects. Predict which ones will float. Then fill a large bowl with water. Put each object in the water. Were your predictions right?

Measuring Liquids

You can measure liquids. You can use a measuring cup to find out how much space a liquid takes up. You can use a balance to measure its mass.

★ **MAIN IDEA AND DETAILS** How can you measure liquids?

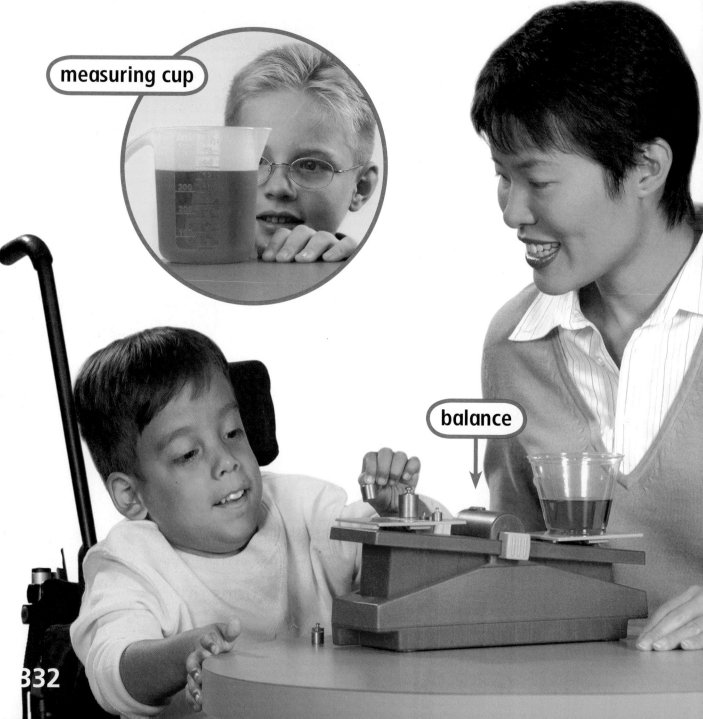

measuring cup

balance

Focus Skill

1. MAIN IDEA AND DETAILS Copy and complete this chart.

Liquids

Main Idea
A liquid is matter that **Ⓐ** _____.
It **Ⓑ** _____ its own shape.

detail
Some matter dissolves in liquids.

detail
Some matter **Ⓒ** _____, and some floats.

2. SUMMARIZE Use the chart to write a lesson summary.

3. VOCABULARY Use **sink** and **float** to talk about this picture.

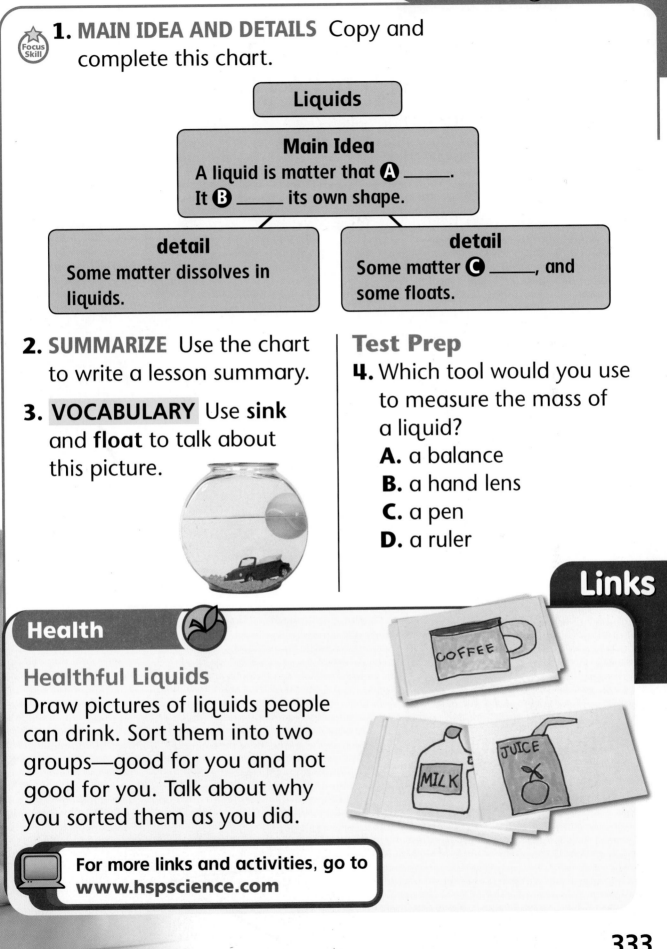

Test Prep

4. Which tool would you use to measure the mass of a liquid?
   A. a balance
   B. a hand lens
   C. a pen
   D. a ruler

Links

Health

Healthful Liquids
Draw pictures of liquids people can drink. Sort them into two groups—good for you and not good for you. Talk about why you sorted them as you did.

COFFEE

MILK   JUICE

💻 **For more links and activities, go to www.hspscience.com**

What Can We Observe About Gases?

Fast Fact

The biggest bubble ever blown was almost as long as three school buses! Look at this bubble. Infer what is inside it.

Matter in a Bottle

You need

- **clean plastic bottle**
- **balloon**

Step 1

Squeeze the bottle. Blow up the balloon. Observe the air coming out of each.

Step 2

Put the balloon in the bottle. Pull the end around the top. Try to blow up the balloon.

Step 3

What happened? **Infer** what else is in the bottle.

Inquiry Skill

When you **infer**, you use what you observed to tell why something happened.

335

VOCABULARY
gas
steam

 READING FOCUS SKILL

CAUSE AND EFFECT Think about how and why matter may change.

Observing Gases

Air is made of gases. A gas is a kind of matter. You can not see most gases.

Where is the air in each picture?

A **gas** is matter that does not have its own shape. It spreads out to fill its container. It takes the shape of the container.

★ Focus Skill **CAUSE AND EFFECT** **What would happen if you blew air into a bag? Why?**

Insta-Lab

A Wind Hunt

Did you know that wind is moving air? Go on an air hunt. Tape yarn to the end of a pencil. Hold it near heaters, windows, and doors. Observe the yarn. What makes it move?

Heating and Cooling Matter

Heating and cooling can change matter. You can see how matter changes by observing water.

In summer the water in this stream is warm. This keeps the water liquid.

water

In winter the water in the stream gets cold. When the water gets cold enough, it changes into ice. Ice is solid water.

In spring the water will get warm again. It will change back into a liquid.

CAUSE AND EFFECT **What changes water from a liquid to a solid?**

ice

What Is Steam?

When water boils, it becomes a gas. This gas is called steam .

1

When the water gets hot enough, it becomes steam. The steam goes into the air.

2

As steam cools, it forms tiny drops of water that make a little cloud.

For more links and activities, go to www.hspscience.com

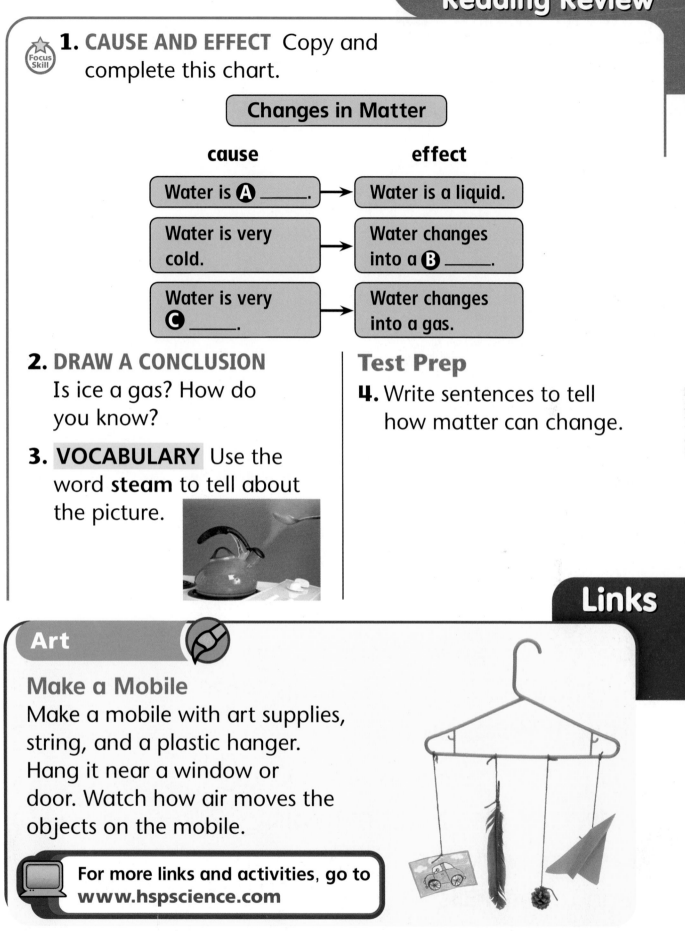

Focus Skill

1. CAUSE AND EFFECT Copy and complete this chart.

Changes in Matter

cause		effect
Water is Ⓐ _____.	→	Water is a liquid.
Water is very cold.	→	Water changes into a Ⓑ _____.
Water is very Ⓒ _____.	→	Water changes into a gas.

2. DRAW A CONCLUSION
Is ice a gas? How do you know?

3. VOCABULARY Use the word **steam** to tell about the picture.

Test Prep
4. Write sentences to tell how matter can change.

Links

Art

Make a Mobile
Make a mobile with art supplies, string, and a plastic hanger. Hang it near a window or door. Watch how air moves the objects on the mobile.

For more links and activities, go to **www.hspscience.com**

341

Cleaning Up Oil

Oil spills can happen when a boat carrying oil hits something. Oil is liquid that does not mix with water. It floats on water.

Oil pollutes water in oceans, lakes, or rivers. It also hurts animals. Scientists worked to find ways to clean up oil spills.

When oil spills into the ocean, it is very hard to clean up. Workers must use special soap and sponges to clean up the oil.

THINK ABOUT IT

How can oil spills harm the environment?

Well Oiled

Oil is a heavy, sticky liquid. Some of it is even used to heat houses.

 Find out more! Log on to **www.hspscience.com**

Making Protective Packages

Have you ever opened a milk carton and a bad smell came out? That is because the milk turned sour. Milk turns sour after about 14 days.

A scientist named Manuel Marquez Sanchez has made a new kind of milk carton. This new carton changes color. It changes color when the milk inside it is turning sour. Sanchez is also trying to make other food packages better.

You Can Do It!

Materials
- water
- 2 ice cube trays
- freezer

Explore Cooling

What to Do

1. Fill both trays with water.
2. Put one tray in a freezer. Put the other on a table.
3. Wait a few hours. Then look at each tray. What happened?

Draw Conclusions
How did the liquid water change in the freezer? Why?

Mixtures All Around

Many things are mixtures. Choose a mixture in your classroom. Draw it. Then look for the different kinds of matter that are in it. Label each kind. Compare your drawing with a classmate's.

Review and Test Preparation

Vocabulary Review

Tell which picture goes best with each word.

1. solid p. 321   **3. liquid** p. 328

2. mass p. 324   **4. float** p. 330

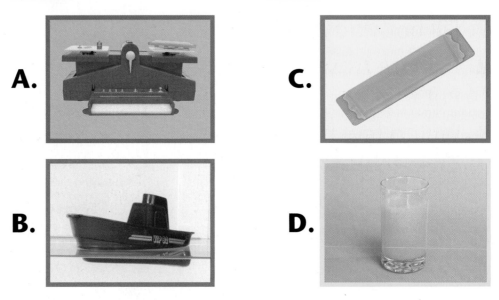

A.

B.

C.

D.

Check Understanding

5. Tell why this is a mixture.

6. Which is a liquid?

    A. air

    B. clay

    C. milk

    D. paper

Critical Thinking

7. What **causes** the stream to change from a solid to a liquid?

8. Think of a solid object. How could you measure it? Write a plan.

UNIT F

Energy in Our World

PHYSICAL SCIENCE

Louisville Slugger Museum

TO: drew@hspscience.com

FROM: harper@hspscience.com

RE: Louisville, Kentucky

Dear Drew,
Jim and I visited a museum. Outside I saw a baseball bat that is taller than the museum!
Harper

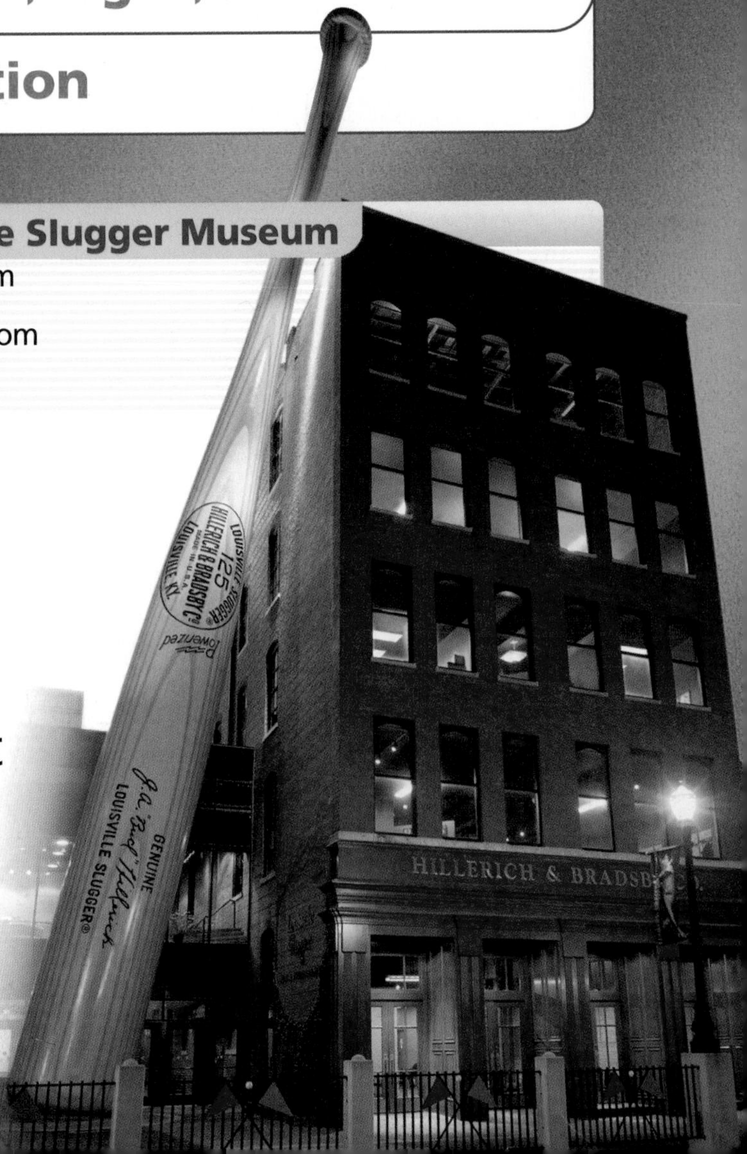

US Olympic Training Center

TO: carly@hspscience.com

FROM: scott@hspscience.com

RE: Colorado Springs, Colorado

Dear Carly,

Do you still like to race your bike?
I visited the Olympic Training
Center. Maybe you will get to
train there someday!
Your big brother,
Scott

Experiment!

Gravity As you do this unit, you will learn how things move. Plan and do a test. Find out how to make a toy truck go farther.

11 Heat, Light, and Sound

Vocabulary

heat	vibrate
light	loudness
shadow	pitch
sound	

I wonder...

Why do musical instruments make different sounds?

What do **YOU** *wonder?*

What Is Heat?

Heat from the Sun

You need

- **cup of soil**

- **2 thermometers**

Step 1

Does the sun warm soil faster than it warms air? **Plan an investigation** to find out. Write your **plan**.

Step 2

Follow your **plan** to **investigate** your ideas.

Step 3

Share with the class what you learned.

Inquiry Skill

You **plan an investigation** by thinking of ideas and trying them out.

READING FOCUS SKILL

CAUSE AND EFFECT Look for all the effects heat has on things.

Heat

Heat is energy that makes things hot. Heat from the sun warms the land, air, and water all around you.

The sun warms land, air, and water.

Some things warm up faster than others. Dark-colored things warm up quickly in the sun. Light-colored things take longer to warm up.

CAUSE AND EFFECT
What can cause something to warm up quickly?

Which part of the street gets hot faster?

355

Other Sources of Heat

You can feel heat from other things, too. Fire gives off heat. Lamps and stoves can give off heat. Moving things give off heat, too. Rub your hands together. What do you feel?

Focus Skill **CAUSE AND EFFECT** What happens when you rub your hands together?

lamp

fire

stove

friction from rubbing hands

Focus Skill

1. CAUSE AND EFFECT Copy and complete this chart.

Heat

cause	effect
The sun makes things hot. →	Land, **A** _____, and water get warm.
A thing is dark-colored. →	It warms up **B** _____.
A thing is **C** _____. →	It warms up slowly.
You rub your hands together. →	They feel **D** _____.

2. SUMMARIZE Use the chart to summarize this lesson.

3. VOCABULARY Tell about the **heat** in this picture.

Test Prep

4. Which things warm up fastest?
  A. big things
  B. cold things
  C. dark-colored things
  D. light-colored things

Links

Writing

Report
Read about the sun. Then write a short report about it. Tell what it is and where it is. Tell what the sun is made of and what it does. Draw pictures to go with your report.

For more links and activities, go to **www.hspscience.com**

The sun is a star.

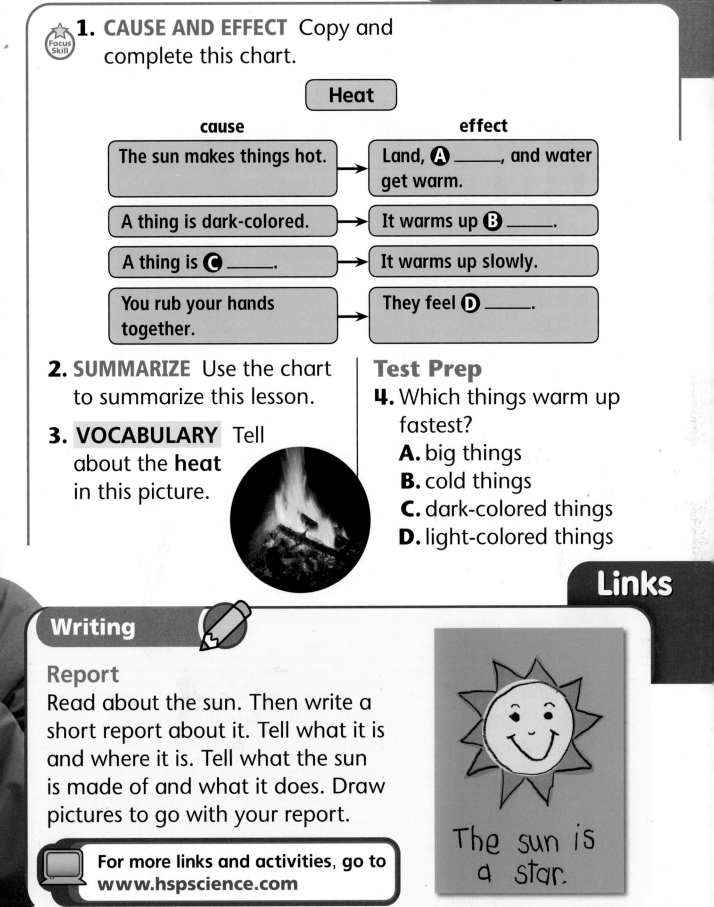

What Can Light Do?

Fast Fact

A shadow has a shape like the object that made it. Draw a conclusion about how shadows are made.

Look at Shadows

You need

- pencil
- clay
- paper
- crayon

Step 1

Put a pencil in clay.
Put it on the paper.
Put it in a sunny place.

Step 2

Trace the shadow you see on the paper. Then trace it at two other times of the day.

Step 3

Draw a conclusion about why the shadow changed.

Inquiry Skill

To **draw a conclusion,** use what you observed and what you already know.

359

VOCABULARY
light
shadow

READING FOCUS SKILL

MAIN IDEA AND DETAILS Look for the main ideas about light and what it does.

Light

Light is a kind of energy. Light from the sun lights up the world around us. Fire and lamps give off light, too. Light lets us see.

sunlight

glass door

closed blinds

Light can move. It can pass through clear objects. It passes through glass. Light can not pass through all objects. Objects that are not clear block light.

⭐ **MAIN IDEA AND DETAILS**
Focus Skill
What is the main thing light does for us?

Insta-Lab

What Can Light Pass Through?

Get some art materials. Predict which ones light will pass through. Which ones will block light? Test your ideas in a sunny place or next to a lamp. **CAUTION:** A lamp may get hot.

Shadows

A **shadow** is a dark place made when an object blocks light. You can see many shadows on a sunny day.

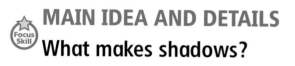

MAIN IDEA AND DETAILS
What makes shadows?

shadow

shadow

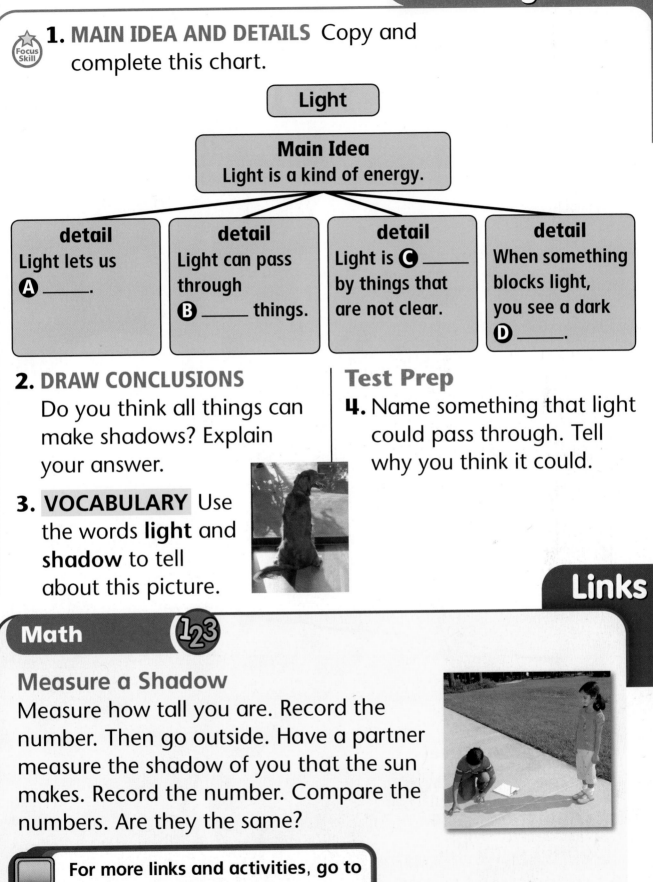

Focus Skill

1. MAIN IDEA AND DETAILS Copy and complete this chart.

Light

Main Idea
Light is a kind of energy.

detail	detail	detail	detail
Light lets us **Ⓐ** ____.	Light can pass through **Ⓑ** ____ things.	Light is **Ⓒ** ____ by things that are not clear.	When something blocks light, you see a dark **Ⓓ** ____.

2. DRAW CONCLUSIONS
Do you think all things can make shadows? Explain your answer.

3. VOCABULARY Use the words **light** and **shadow** to tell about this picture.

Test Prep
4. Name something that light could pass through. Tell why you think it could.

Links

Math

Measure a Shadow
Measure how tall you are. Record the number. Then go outside. Have a partner measure the shadow of you that the sun makes. Record the number. Compare the numbers. Are they the same?

For more links and activities, go to **www.hspscience.com**

What Is Sound?

Fast Fact

Sound can travel across spaces. You can hypothesize about what helps sound travel.

Watching Sound

You need

• rice   • bowl with foil   • pan   • spoon

Step 1

Put a little rice on the foil. **Hypothesize**. Tell what you think will happen to the rice if you make a loud sound.

Step 2

Hold the pan next to the bowl. Tap it once with the spoon. Observe the rice.

Step 3

Was your **hypothesis** right? Talk about it.

Inquiry Skill

To **hypothesize**, tell what you think will happen. Then test your idea.

Reading in Science

VOCABULARY

sound
vibrate
loudness
pitch

READING FOCUS SKILL

COMPARE AND CONTRAST Look for ways sounds can be alike and different.

How Sounds Are Made

Sound is a kind of energy that you hear. It is made when something vibrates. To **vibrate** is to move quickly back and forth.

What sounds do you think you could hear on this street?

When you strum
guitar strings, each string
vibrates. It makes a sound
that you can hear.

COMPARE AND CONTRAST
How are all sounds alike?

homemade guitar

vibrating strings

guitar

Sounds Are Different

Some sounds are soft, and some are loud. A sound's **loudness** is how loud or soft it is. The jet makes a loud sound. What else makes a loud sound?

Whispers are soft sounds.

Jets make loud sounds.

368

Some sounds are high. Others are low. A sound's **pitch** is how high or low it is. The big bell has a low pitch. What else has a low pitch?

 COMPARE AND CONTRAST
What is one way sounds may be different?

Insta-Lab

Straw Instrument
Cut a straw so that the top forms a V. Pinch the top with your lips. Blow very hard. Listen. Then cut some of the bottom off the straw. Blow again. How does the sound change?

Some wind chimes have a high pitch.

A big bell has a low pitch.

Musical Instruments

Musical instruments are objects people use to make music. Each kind of instrument causes air to vibrate to make sounds.

When you blow into a trumpet, air vibrates in its metal tubes.

A saxophone has a wooden part called a reed. The reed vibrates, as does the air inside the instrument.

A violin has strings that vibrate.

A drum has a tough cover that vibrates.

For more links and activities, go to www.hspscience.com

Focus Skill

1. COMPARE AND CONTRAST Copy and complete this chart.

Sound

alike

All sounds are made when something **A** _____.

different

A sound's loudness can be loud or **B** _____.

A sound's pitch can be high or **C** _____.

2. SUMMARIZE Use the chart to write a summary of the lesson.

3. VOCABULARY Use the word **vibrate** to tell about the picture.

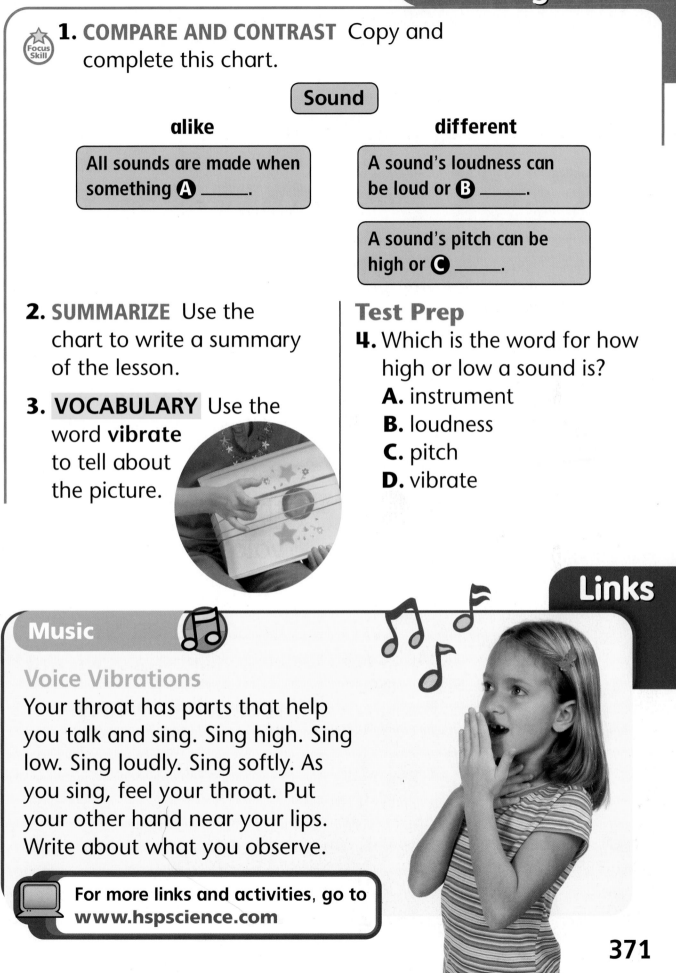

Test Prep

4. Which is the word for how high or low a sound is?
  A. instrument
  B. loudness
  C. pitch
  D. vibrate

Links

Music

Voice Vibrations
Your throat has parts that help you talk and sing. Sing high. Sing low. Sing loudly. Sing softly. As you sing, feel your throat. Put your other hand near your lips. Write about what you observe.

For more links and activities, go to www.hspscience.com

How Cell Phones Work

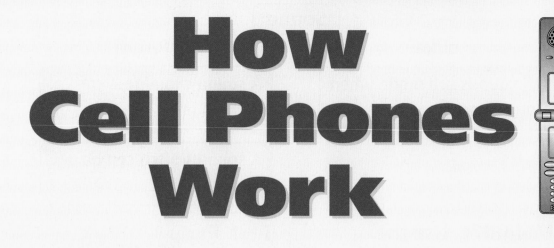

Have you seen kids with cell phones? A cell phone is really a radio. It turns the sound of your voice into another kind of energy. This energy then travels through the air until it reaches a tower.

Dialing Out

The tower picks up the energy. Then the tower sends it out to the number you dialed.

The other person's phone turns the energy back into sound. Did you ever think you would be talking through the air?

THINK ABOUT IT

What does a cell phone do to your voice when you talk into it?

Find out more! Log on to **www.hspscience.com**

Lighting the World

Thomas Alva Edison was a scientist. He was also an inventor. As a boy he did not hear well. He spent a lot of time reading. Edison loved to read the many science books his mother gave him.

Edison made a special light bulb. The bulb had a special thread inside of it. It could stay lit longer than other light bulbs. Soon his light bulb glowed in many places. Thomas Edison had changed our world.

You Can Do It!

Investigate Pitch
What to Do

1. Blow across the open top of a bottle. Listen. Predict how the sound will change if you put water in the bottle.

2. Put a different amount in each bottle. Blow across the four bottles.

3. Which have a high pitch? Which have a low pitch? Arrange the bottles from highest to lowest pitch.

Materials
- four bottles
- water

Draw Conclusions
What vibrates in an empty bottle to make sound? What effect does adding water have on the sound?

Sun Catcher

Cut out shapes from art materials. Glue them to a sheet of clear colored material. Then hang the sheet in a sunny window. Watch your sun catcher.

375

Review and Test Preparation

Vocabulary Review

Match each word to its picture.

1. heat p. 354 **A.**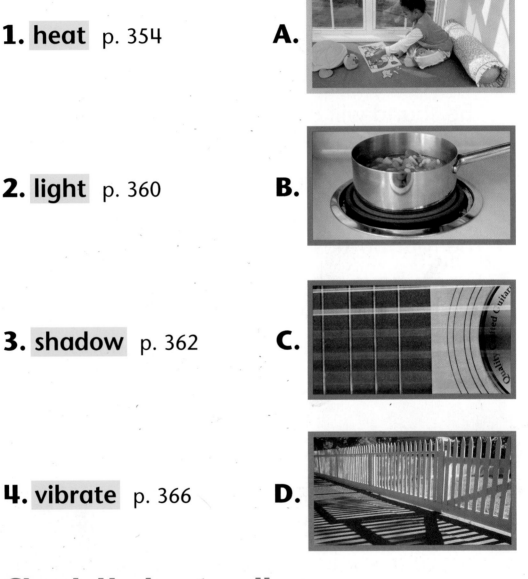

2. light p. 360 **B.**

3. shadow p. 362 **C.**

4. vibrate p. 366 **D.**

Check Understanding

5. What **causes** some things to warm up faster than others?

6. Which clothes are good to wear on a hot day? Tell why.

7. Which kind of pitch does a whistle have?

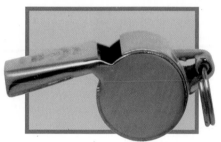

A. high

B. loud

C. low

D. soft

Critical Thinking

8. Look at this musical instrument. What parts vibrate to make sounds? How do you know?

Vocabulary

motion	magnet
speed	attract
force	magnetic force
push	pole
pull	repel
gravity	

I wonder...

What makes a roller coaster move?

What do YOU wonder?

How Do Things Move?

Ways Objects Move

You need

- **objects**

Step 1

Move each object. Observe the way it moves.

Step 2

Classify the objects by the ways they move. Then write about the groups you made.

Step 3

Talk with classmates about your groups. Compare your results.

Inquiry Skill

Classify the objects by grouping those that move the same way.

381

VOCABULARY
motion
speed

READING FOCUS SKILL
COMPARE AND CONTRAST Look for ways motion and speed can be alike and different.

Motion

Things are in motion all around you. When something is in **motion**, it is moving. What is moving here?

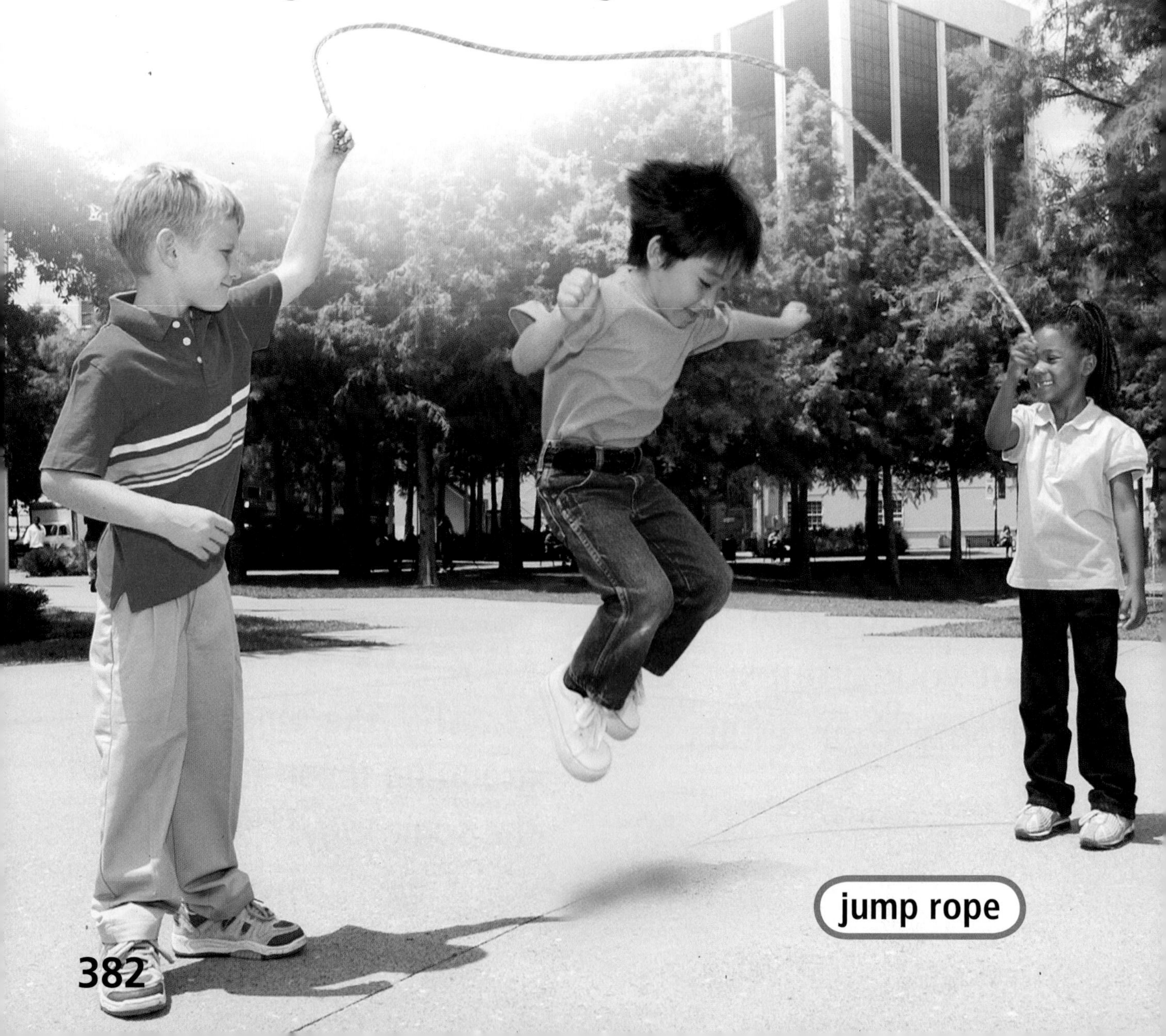

jump rope

race car

Objects move at different speeds. **Speed** is how fast something moves. Both of these objects are moving. They are not moving at the same speed. Which is moving faster?

⭐ Focus Skill **COMPARE AND CONTRAST** How can speeds of objects be different?

tricycle

Motion Graph

Test some toys. Do they move in a straight path, a curved path, a circle, or a zigzag? Record. Then make a bar graph to show how many toys move in each way.

How Things Move

Things may move in different ways. An object may move in a straight path. It may move in a curved path. It may go in a circle. It may even move in a zigzag.

zigzag

★ **COMPARE AND CONTRAST**

What are some different ways an object can move?

curved path

circle

straight path

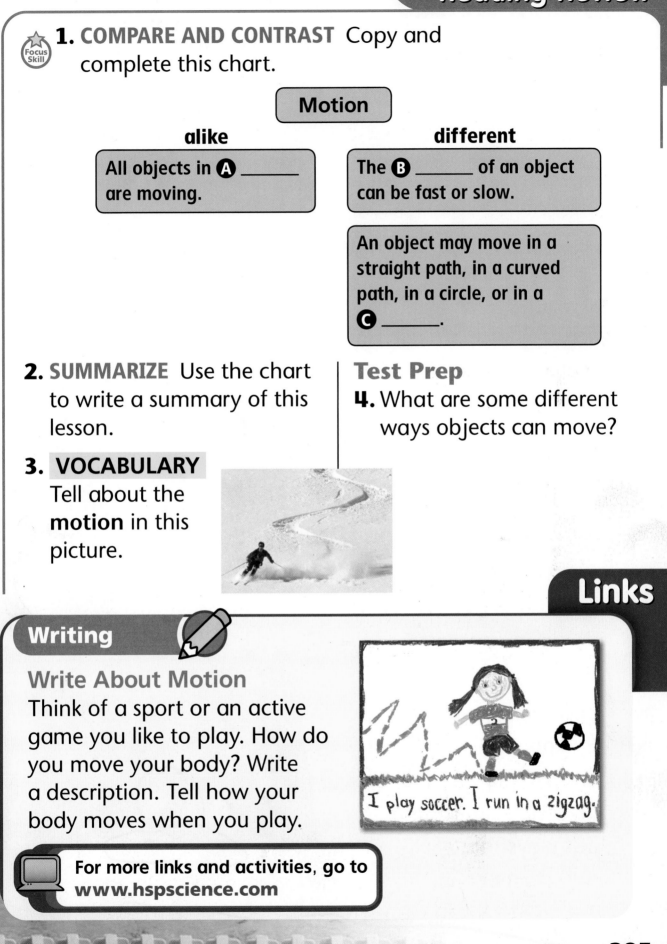

Focus Skill

1. COMPARE AND CONTRAST Copy and complete this chart.

Motion

alike

All objects in **Ⓐ** _____ are moving.

different

The **Ⓑ** _____ of an object can be fast or slow.

An object may move in a straight path, in a curved path, in a circle, or in a **Ⓒ** _____.

2. SUMMARIZE Use the chart to write a summary of this lesson.

3. VOCABULARY Tell about the **motion** in this picture.

Test Prep

4. What are some different ways objects can move?

Links

Writing

Write About Motion

Think of a sport or an active game you like to play. How do you move your body? Write a description. Tell how your body moves when you play.

I play soccer. I run in a zigzag.

For more links and activities, go to **www.hspscience.com**

How Can You Change the Way Things Move?

This man is a juggler. He can juggle 3 pins at a time. You can plan an investigation to find out ways to make objects move.

386

Pulling and Pushing Objects

You need

- **small cube**
- **objects to make cube move**

Step 1

Look at the objects. How can you use them to push or pull the cube? **Plan an investigation**.

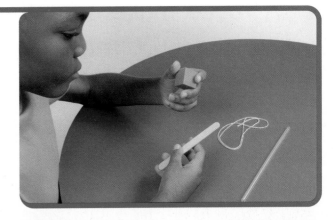

Step 2

Follow your **plan**. Tell how you moved the cube. Use the words push and pull.

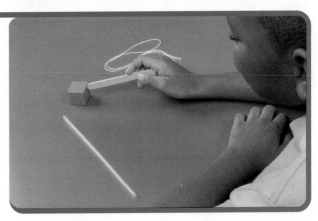

Step 3

Repeat your **plan**. Do you get the same results?

Inquiry Skill

You can **plan an investigation**. Think of ways to move the cube, and then try them.

VOCABULARY
force
push
pull

READING FOCUS SKILL

CAUSE AND EFFECT Look for actions that cause objects to move.

Making Things Move

A **force** makes something move or stop moving. You use force each time you move an object. You use force to move your body, too.

Pushes and pulls are forces. When you **push** an object, you move it away from you. When you **pull** an object, you move it closer to you.

⭐ **Focus Skill** **CAUSE AND EFFECT** What happens when you push an object?

pulling

pushing

389

Changing Speed

You use force to change the speed of an object. These balls are moving very fast. You can push to stop a ball. Then you can pull it close. You can also push it away by kicking to make it move faster.

CAUSE AND EFFECT What may cause a ball to move faster?

pulling toward

pushing away

Changing Direction

You use force to change an object's direction. When you play baseball, the ball moves toward you. Then you hit it with the bat. Hitting the ball is a push. The ball moves away from you.

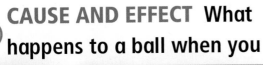 **CAUSE AND EFFECT** What happens to a ball when you hit it?

Insta-Lab

Push and Pull a Ball

Play ball with classmates. Throw and kick a ball to one another. Each time you touch the ball, tell whether you use a push or a pull.

What force does the boy use to change the ball's direction?

391

Changing Position

You use force to change where an object is. You can pull part of a toy truck up and push part of it down. You can push a toy truck inside the station and pull it outside. You can push it forward and pull it backward.

 CAUSE AND EFFECT How can you change where an object is?

up and down

inside and outside

forward and backward

1. CAUSE AND EFFECT Copy and complete this chart.

cause   effects

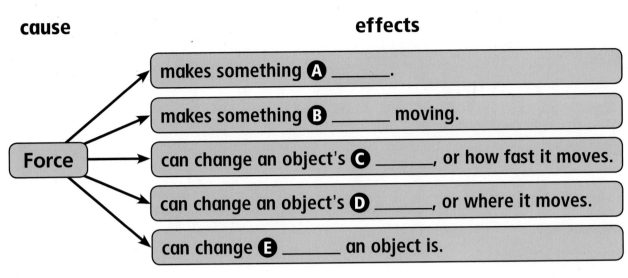

Force

makes something **A** _____.

makes something **B** _____ moving.

can change an object's **C** _____, or how fast it moves.

can change an object's **D** _____, or where it moves.

can change **E** _____ an object is.

2. DRAW CONCLUSIONS What force do you use when you jump?

3. VOCABULARY Use the word **push** to tell about the picture.

Test Prep

4. Write a sentence about what causes objects to move or stop moving.

Links

Math

Adding to Keep Score
In some games, players push objects to score points. Make your own pushing game. Use a box lid. Push a bottle cap from one end to score points. Do this 3 times. Add your points to find your score.

 For more links and activities, go to www.hspscience.com

How Does Gravity Make Things Move?

Fast Fact

Gravity pulls your body down a slide. You can predict how gravity will move an object.

How a Ball Will Move

You need

• tape

• ball

• ramp

Step 1

Set up the ramp. **Predict** where the ball will stop when you roll it down the ramp. Mark the spot with tape.

Step 2

Roll the ball down the ramp.

Step 3

Was your **prediction** correct? Talk about what you found out.

Inquiry Skill

To **predict** where the ball will go, think about how a ball moves.

(Focus Skill) **READING FOCUS SKILL**
CAUSE AND EFFECT Look for the effect gravity has on objects.

Gravity Makes Things Move

Gravity is a force that pulls things straight down to the ground. It makes things fall unless something is holding them up.

Look at the diver. Nothing is holding her up. Which way will she move? The diver will move down, because of gravity.

(Focus Skill) **CAUSE AND EFFECT** What effect does gravity have on objects?

diver →

dog food

What is gravity moving here?

sled

Insta-Lab

Falling Objects

Watch the way gravity pulls different things down. Your teacher will drop a ball and a pencil from high up. Observe how they fall. Why do you think this happened?

397

How Things Fall

Gravity moves all objects on Earth the same way. It pulls them straight down. A push or a pull can change an object's path. A push or a pull can hold an object up. If there are no pushes or pulls, all objects fall.

The ball is light. The rock is heavy.

The boy drops the ball and the rock at the same time.

Both fall and land at the same time.

For more links and activities, go to www.hspscience.com

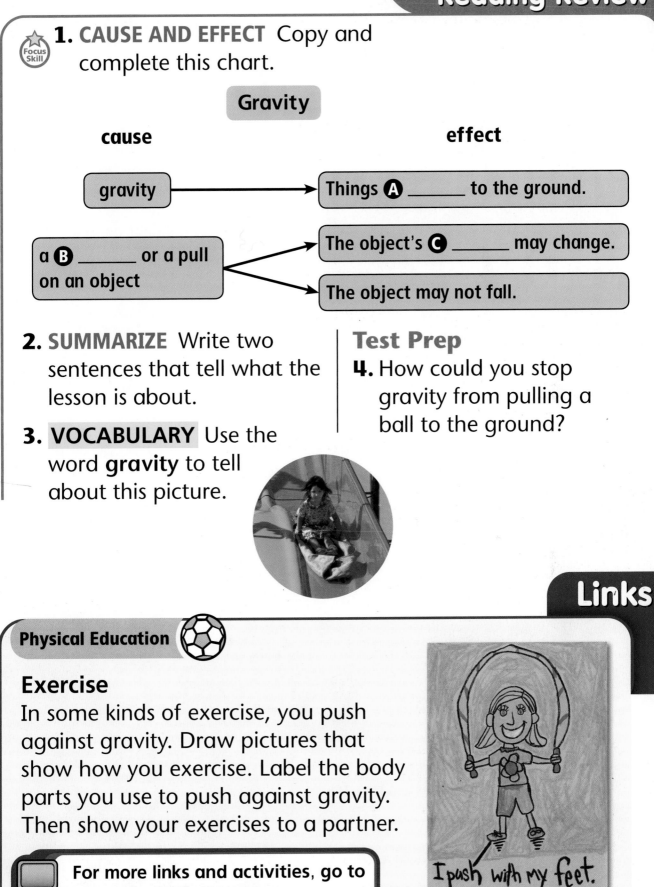

1. CAUSE AND EFFECT Copy and complete this chart.

Gravity

cause

effect

gravity → Things **A** _____ to the ground.

a **B** _____ or a pull on an object → The object's **C** _____ may change.

The object may not fall.

2. SUMMARIZE Write two sentences that tell what the lesson is about.

3. VOCABULARY Use the word **gravity** to tell about this picture.

Test Prep

4. How could you stop gravity from pulling a ball to the ground?

Links

Physical Education

Exercise

In some kinds of exercise, you push against gravity. Draw pictures that show how you exercise. Label the body parts you use to push against gravity. Then show your exercises to a partner.

For more links and activities, go to www.hspscience.com

I push with my feet.

How Do Magnets Make Things Move?

Fast Fact

This magnet is very strong.
It can pick up recycled steel.
You can hypothesize about
what a magnet will pull.

What Magnets Pull

You need

- **bar magnet**
- **objects**

Step 1

Look at the objects.
Which ones will
a magnet pull?
Hypothesize.

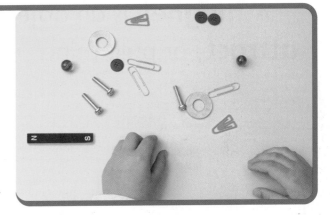

Step 2

Test your **hypothesis**.
Use a magnet. Record
your observations.

What a Magnet Can Do		
Object	Pulls	Does Not Pull

Step 3

Was your **hypothesis**
correct? How do
you know?

Inquiry Skill

When you **hypothesize**,
you think of an idea.

401

VOCABULARY

magnet   pole
attract   repel
magnetic force

⭐ **READING FOCUS SKILL**

MAIN IDEA AND DETAILS Find out what magnets are and how they move objects.

Magnets

A **magnet** is an object that will **attract**, or pull, things made of iron.

magnets

What does a magnet attract?
You can test objects to see. A magnet
does not attract all metals. It attracts
metals that have iron in them. Steel
has iron in it.

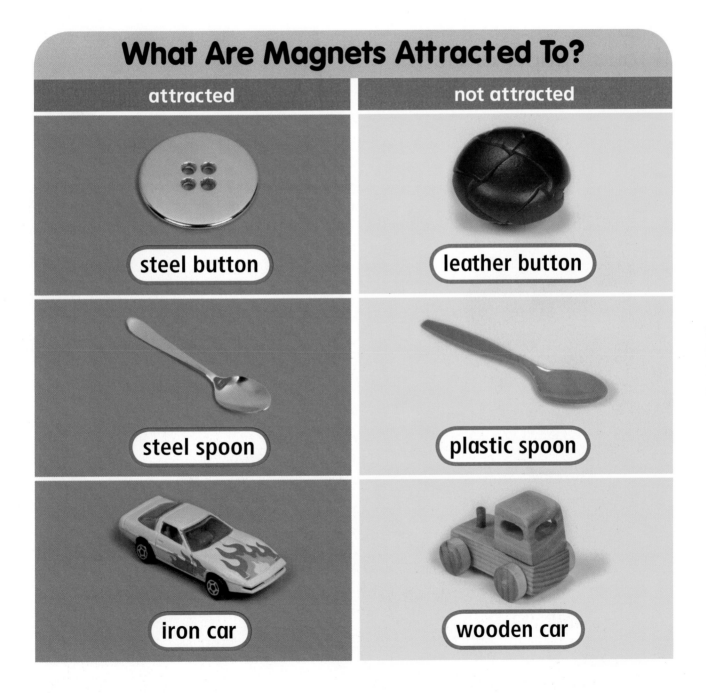

What Are Magnets Attracted To?

attracted	not attracted
steel button	leather button
steel spoon	plastic spoon
iron car	wooden car

MAIN IDEA AND DETAILS What is a magnet?

Force of a Magnet

A magnet's pull is called **magnetic force**. Some magnets have a lot of force. They are very strong. Many magnets can even pull through paper or cloth.

magnet pulling through paper

magnet pulling without touching

Magnets attract objects without touching them. Strong ones can pull from far away. This magnet pulls a paper clip on a kite when it is held above it.

⭐ **MAIN IDEA AND DETAILS**
How do you know if a magnet has a strong magnetic force?

Insta-Lab

Move It With a Magnet
Find out what a magnet pulls through. Use a strong magnet. Try to attract a metal clip through paper, cloth, and other materials. Tell what you observe.

Poles of a Magnet

A magnet has an N pole and an S pole. A **pole** is near an end of a bar magnet. The pull is strongest at a magnet's poles.

You can try to put magnets together. If the poles are different, they attract each other. Poles that are the same **repel** each other, or push each other away.

 MAIN IDEA AND DETAILS
What are a magnet's poles?

poles

What happens when you try to put magnets together?

Focus Skill

1. **MAIN IDEA AND DETAILS** Copy and complete this chart.

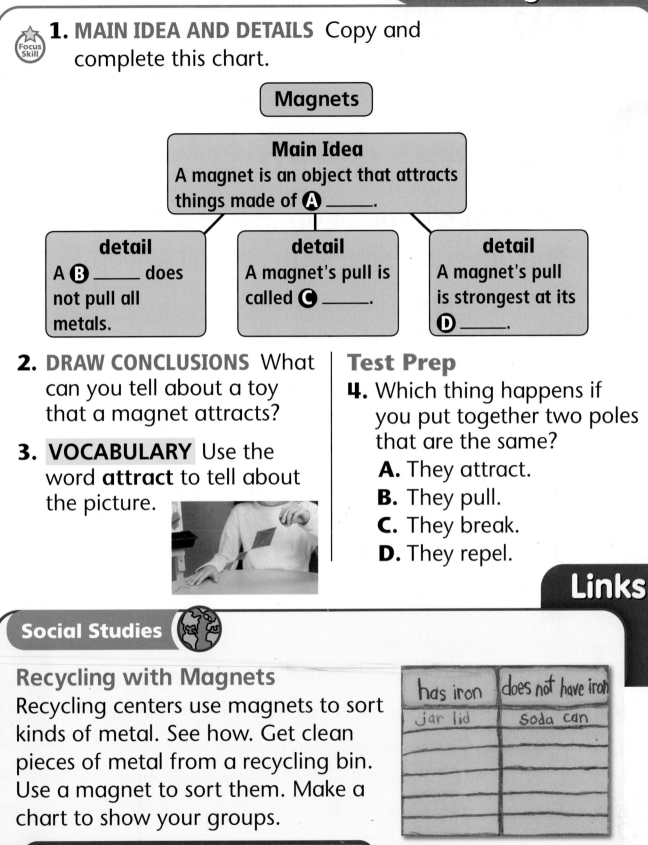

Magnets

Main Idea
A magnet is an object that attracts things made of **A** _____.

detail
A **B** _____ does not pull all metals.

detail
A magnet's pull is called **C** _____.

detail
A magnet's pull is strongest at its **D** _____.

2. **DRAW CONCLUSIONS** What can you tell about a toy that a magnet attracts?

3. **VOCABULARY** Use the word **attract** to tell about the picture.

Test Prep

4. Which thing happens if you put together two poles that are the same?
   A. They attract.
   B. They pull.
   C. They break.
   D. They repel.

Links

Social Studies

Recycling with Magnets
Recycling centers use magnets to sort kinds of metal. See how. Get clean pieces of metal from a recycling bin. Use a magnet to sort them. Make a chart to show your groups.

has iron	does not have iron
jar lid	soda can

For more links and activities, go to www.hspscience.com

Making Driving Safer

It is late at night on a dark road. The driver of a car starts to fall asleep. Then, snap! The seatbelt gets tight. It wakes up the driver!

In the past, people did not worry about falling asleep. They used wagons and horses to get places. Then cars took the place of the wagons. These cars were slow. The cars got faster over time.

Driving on roads these days is not very safe. Drivers need to be more careful than ever. This seatbelt is one new tool that keeps drivers safe.

THINK ABOUT IT

Why would a car that goes faster be less safe?

  Find out more! Log on to
www.hspscience.com

Moving with Magnets

John Fowler is learning about magnets. He learned that a magnet can pick up things that have iron in them.

John took a magnet off the refrigerator at home. He used it to try to pick up things around the house.

John picked up paper clips. He dropped one in a glass. The magnet even pulled the paper clip through glass and water!

You Can Do It!

Make a Magnetic Toy

What to Do

1. Cut a small kite from tissue paper.

2. Tie a paper clip to a thread. Tape the clip to the kite. Tape the end of the thread to a table.

3. Hold the magnet above the kite but not touching the kite. Can you use the magnet to make your kite fly?

Materials
- scissors
- thread
- tissue paper
- paper clip
- tape
- magnet

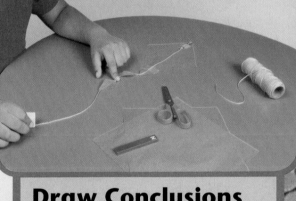

Draw Conclusions
What part of the kite does the magnet pull? Why?

Wheel Hunt

How are a bicycle, a car, and skates alike? They have wheels. Wheels help objects move. Look around for objects with wheels. Tell how each one moves.

411

Review and Test Preparation

Vocabulary Review

Choose the word that best completes each sentence.

speed p. 383   **magnet** p. 402

gravity p. 396   **repel** p. 406

1. For a magnet, to push away is to ___.

2. An object that attracts things made of iron is a ___.

3. A force that pulls things to the ground is ___.

4. How fast an object moves is its ___.

Check Understanding

5. Use these pictures to **compare** different ways objects can move.

6. Look at this picture. What is **causing** the sled to move?

   A. gravity
   B. magnetic force
   C. N and S poles
   D. speed

Critical Thinking

7. Why do you think magnets stick to most refrigerators?

8. List these objects in order from slowest to fastest.

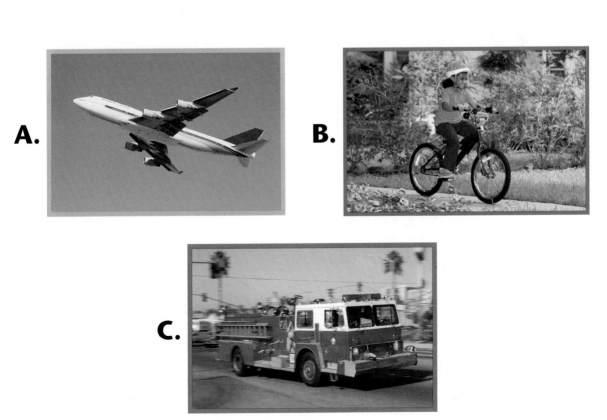

A.

B.

C.

References

Contents

Health Handbook

Reading in Science Handbook

Math in Science Handbook — R20

Your Senses

You have five senses that tell you about the world. Your five senses are sight, hearing, smell, taste, and touch.

Your Eyes

If you look at your eyes in a mirror, you will see an outer white part, a colored part called the iris, and a dark hole in the middle. This hole is called the pupil.

Caring for Your Eyes

- Have a doctor check your eyes to find out if they are healthy.

- Never look directly at the sun or at very bright lights.

- Wear sunglasses outdoors in bright sunlight and on snow and water.

- Don't touch or rub your eyes.

- Protect your eyes when you play sports.

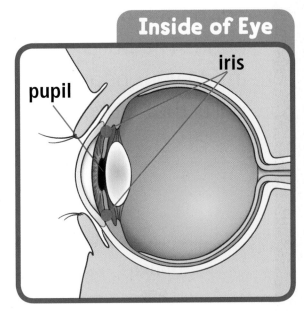

Inside of Eye

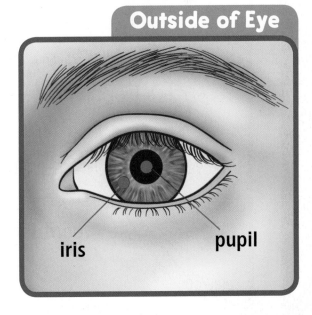

Outside of Eye

Your Senses

Your Ears

Your ears let you hear the things around you. You can see only a small part of the ear on the outside of your head. The parts of your ear inside your head are the parts that let you hear.

Caring for Your Ears

- Have a doctor check your ears.

- Avoid very loud noises.

- Never put anything in your ears.

- Protect your ears when you play sports.

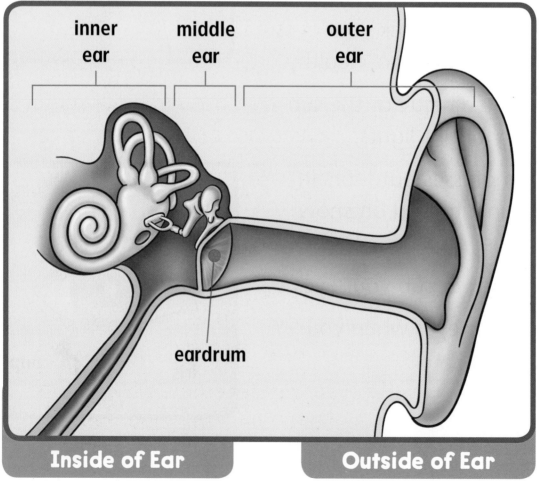

| inner ear | middle ear | outer ear |

eardrum

Inside of Ear   **Outside of Ear**

Your Senses of Smell and Taste

Your nose cleans the air you breathe and lets you smell things. Your nose and tongue help you taste things you eat and drink.

Your Skin

Your skin protects your body from germs. Your skin also gives you your sense of touch.

Caring for Your Skin

• Always wash your hands after coughing or blowing your nose, touching an animal, playing outside, or using the restroom.

• Protect your skin from sunburn. Wear a hat and clothes to cover your skin outdoors.

• Use sunscreen to protect your skin from the sun.

• Wear proper safety pads and a helmet when you play sports, ride a bike, or skate.

Your Skeletal System

Inside your body are many hard, strong bones. They form your skeletal system. The bones in your body protect parts inside your body.

Your skeletal system works with your muscular system to hold your body up and to give it shape.

Caring for Your Skeletal System

- Always wear a helmet and other safety gear when you skate, ride a bike or a scooter, or play sports.

- Eat foods that help keep your bones strong and hard.

- Exercise to help your bones stay strong and healthy.

- Get plenty of rest to help your bones grow.

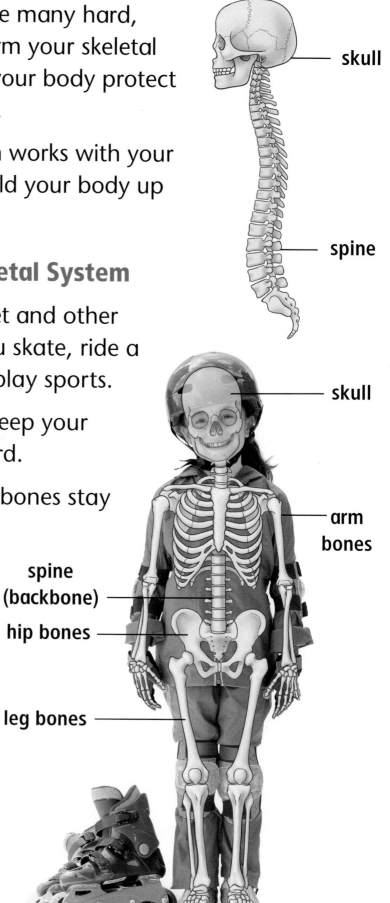

skull

spine

skull

arm bones

spine (backbone)

hip bones

leg bones

Your Muscular System

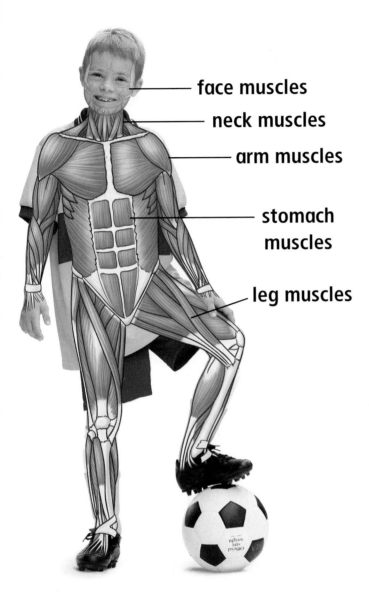

face muscles

neck muscles

arm muscles

stomach muscles

leg muscles

Your muscular system is made up of the muscles in your body. Muscles are body parts that help you move.

Caring for Your Muscular System

- Exercise to keep your muscles strong.

- Eat foods that will help your muscles grow.

- Drink plenty of water when you play sports or exercise.

- Rest your muscles after you exercise or play sports.

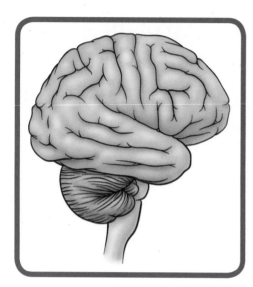

Your brain and your nerves are parts of your nervous system. Your brain keeps your body working. It tells you about the world around you. Your brain also lets you think, remember, and have feelings.

Caring for Your Nervous System

- Get plenty of sleep. Sleeping lets your brain rest.

- Always wear a helmet to protect your head and your brain when you ride a bike or play sports.

Your Digestive System

Your digestive system helps your body get energy from the foods you eat. Your body needs energy to do things.

When your body digests food, it breaks the food down. Your digestive system keeps the things your body needs. It also gets rid of the things your body does not need to keep.

Caring for Your Digestive System

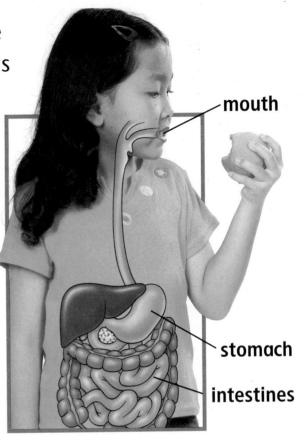
mouth

stomach

intestines

• Brush and floss your teeth every day.

• Wash your hands before you eat.

• Eat slowly and chew your food well before you swallow.

• Eat vegetables and fruits. They help move foods through your digestive system.

Your Respiratory System

You breathe using your respiratory system. Your mouth, nose, and lungs are all parts of your respiratory system.

Caring for Your Respiratory System

• Never put anything in your nose.

• Never smoke.

• Exercise enough to make you breathe harder. Breathing harder makes your lungs stronger.

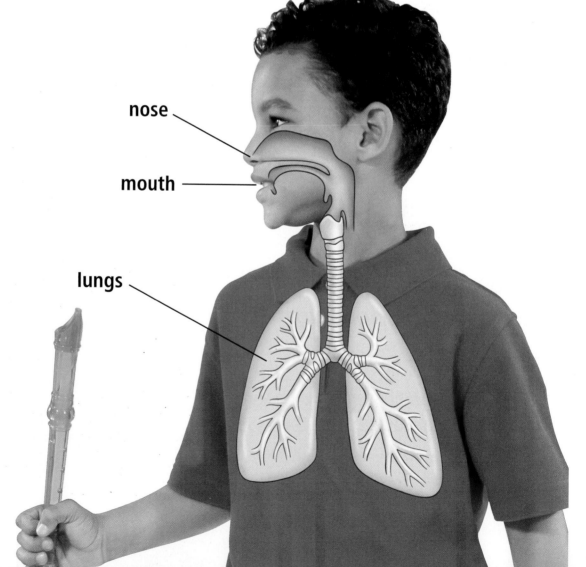

nose

mouth

lungs

Your Circulatory System

Your circulatory system is made up of your heart and your blood vessels. Your blood carries food energy and oxygen to help your body work. Blood vessels are small tubes. They carry blood from your heart to every part of your body.

Your heart is a muscle. It is beating all the time. As your heart beats, it pumps blood through your blood vessels.

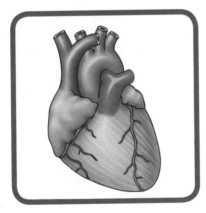

Caring for Your Circulatory System

• Exercise every day to keep your heart strong.

• Eat meats and green leafy vegetables. They help your blood carry oxygen.

• Never touch anyone else's blood.

Staying Healthy

You can do many things to help yourself stay fit and healthy.

You can also avoid doing things that can harm you.

If you know ways to stay safe and healthy and you do these things, you can help yourself have good health.

Getting enough rest

Staying away from alcohol, tobacco, and other drugs

Staying active

Keeping clean

SOAP

Eating right

Keeping Clean

Keeping clean helps you stay healthy. You can pick up germs from the things you touch. Washing with soap and water helps remove germs from your skin.

Wash your hands for as long as it takes to say your ABCs. Always wash your hands at these times.

- Before and after you eat
- After coughing or blowing your nose
- After using the restroom
- After touching an animal
- After playing outside

Caring for Your Teeth

Brushing your teeth and gums keeps them clean and healthy. You should brush your teeth at least twice a day. Brush in the morning. Brush before you go to bed at night. It is also good to brush your teeth after you eat if you can.

Brushing Your Teeth

Use a soft toothbrush that is the right size for you. Always use your own toothbrush. Use only a small amount of toothpaste. It should be about the size of a pea. Be sure to rinse your mouth with water after you brush your teeth.

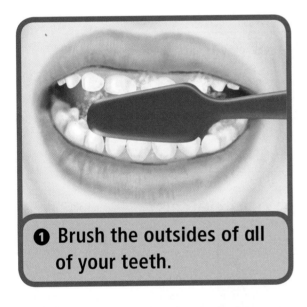

❶ Brush the outsides of all of your teeth.

❷ Brush the insides of all of your teeth.

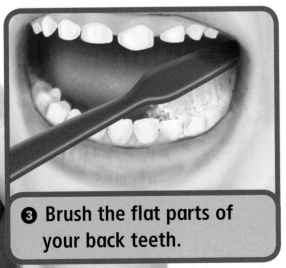

❸ Brush the flat parts of your back teeth.

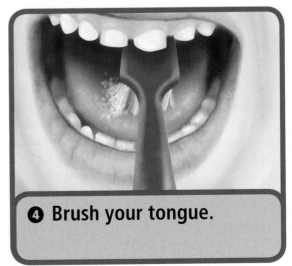

❹ Brush your tongue.

Identify the Main Idea and Details

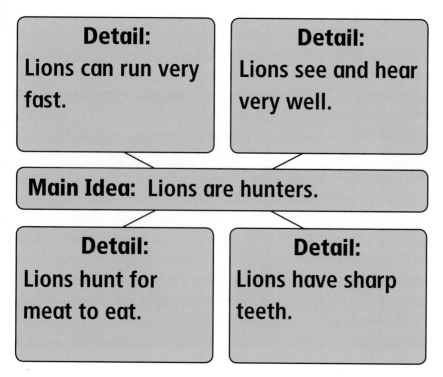

Some lessons in this science book are written to help you find the main idea. Learning how to find the main idea can help you understand what you read. The main idea of a paragraph is what it is mostly about. The details tell you more about it.

Read this paragraph.

> Lions are hunters. They hunt for meat to eat. Lions can run very fast. They see and hear very well. They need sharp teeth to catch animals. They have sharp teeth to eat the meat they catch.

This chart shows the main idea and details.

Detail:
Lions can run very fast.

Detail:
Lions see and hear very well.

Main Idea: Lions are hunters.

Detail:
Lions hunt for meat to eat.

Detail:
Lions have sharp teeth.

Compare and Contrast

(Focus Skill)

Some science lessons are written to help you see how things are alike and different. Learning how to compare and contrast can help you understand what you read.

Read this paragraph.

> Birds and mammals are kinds of animals. Birds have a body covering of feathers. Mammals have a body covering of fur. Both birds and mammals need food, air, and water to live. Most birds can fly. Most mammals walk or run.

Here is how you can compare and contrast birds and mammals.

Ways They Are Alike	**Ways They Are Different**
Compare	Contrast
Both are kinds of animals. Both need food, air, and water to live.	Birds have feathers. Mammals have fur. Most birds fly. Most mammals walk or run.

Some science lessons are written to help you understand why things happen. You can use a chart like this to help you find cause and effect.

Cause		Effect
A cause is why something happens.	→	An effect is what happens.

Some paragraphs have more than one cause or effect. Read this paragraph.

> Water can be a solid, a liquid, or a gas. When water is very cold it turns into solid ice. When water is heated, it turns into water vapor, a gas.

This chart shows two causes and their effects in the paragraph.

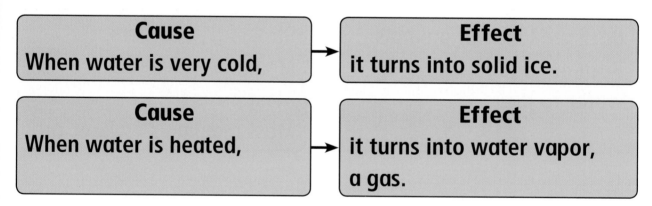

Cause		Effect
When water is very cold,	→	it turns into solid ice.
When water is heated,	→	it turns into water vapor, a gas.

Sequence

Learning how to find sequence can help you understand what you read. You can use a chart like this to help you find sequence.

1. The first step. →	**2. The next step.** →	**3. The last step.**

Some paragraphs use words that help you understand order. Read this paragraph. Look at the underlined words.

> Each day <u>begins</u> when the sun appears. <u>Then</u> the sun slowly climbs into the sky. At midday, the sun is straight overhead. <u>Then</u> the sun slowly falls back to the horizon. At <u>last</u>, the sun is gone. It is nighttime.

This chart shows the sequence of the paragraph.

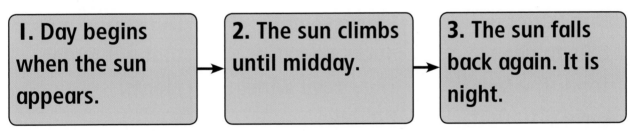

1. Day begins when the sun appears. →	**2. The sun climbs until midday.** →	**3. The sun falls back again. It is night.**

R17

Draw Conclusions

At the end of some lessons, you will be asked to draw conclusions. When you draw conclusions, you tell what you have learned. What you learned also includes your own ideas.

Read this paragraph.

> Birds use their bills to help them get food. Each kind of bird has its own kind of bill. Birds that eat seeds have strong, short bills. Birds that eat bugs have long, sharp bills. Birds that eat water plants have wide, flat bills.

This chart shows how you can draw conclusions.

What I Read		**What I Know**		**Conclusion:**
Birds use their bills to get food. The bills have different shapes.	+	I have seen ducks up close. They have wide, flat bills.	=	Ducks are birds that eat water plants.

 # Summarize

At the end of some lessons, you will be asked to summarize what you read. In a summary, some sentences tell the main idea. Some sentences tell details.

Read this paragraph.

> Honey is made by bees. They gather nectar from flowers. Then they fly home to their beehive with the nectar inside special honey stomachs. The bees put the nectar into special honeycomb holes. Then the bees wait. Soon the nectar will change into sweet, sticky honey. The bees cover the holes with wax that they make. They eat some of the honey during the cold winter.

This chart shows how to summarize what the paragraph is about.

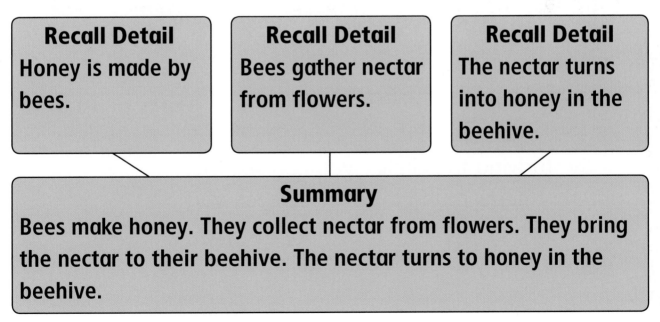

Recall Detail
Honey is made by bees.

Recall Detail
Bees gather nectar from flowers.

Recall Detail
The nectar turns into honey in the beehive.

Summary
Bees make honey. They collect nectar from flowers. They bring the nectar to their beehive. The nectar turns to honey in the beehive.

Using Tables, Charts, and Graphs

Gather Data

When you investigate in science, you need to collect data.

Suppose you want to find out what kinds of things are in soil. You can sort the things you find into groups.

Things I Found in One Cup of Soil

Parts of Plants

Small Rocks

Parts of Animals

By studying the circles, you can see the different items found in soil. However, you might display the data in a different way. For example, you could use a tally table.

Reading a Tally Table

You can show your data in a tally table.

Things I Found in ———— Title
One Cup of Soil

Items Found	Tally
Parts of Plants	⊮	———— Tally marks
Parts of Animals	|||
Small Rocks	⊮ ||

Data

How to Read a Tally Table

1. **Read** the tally table. Use the labels.

2. **Study** the data.

3. **Count** the tally marks.

4. **Draw conclusions**. Ask yourself questions like the ones on this page.

Skills Practice

1. How many parts of plants were found in the soil?

2. How many more small rocks were found in the soil than parts of animals?

3. How many parts of plants and parts of animals were found?

Using Tables, Charts, and Graphs

Reading a Bar Graph

People keep many kinds of animals as pets. This bar graph shows the animal groups pets belong to. A bar graph can be used to compare data.

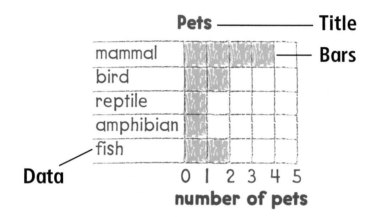

Pets —————— Title

Bars

mammal
bird
reptile
amphibian
fish

Data

0 1 2 3 4 5
number of pets

How to Read a Bar Graph

1. **Look** at the title to learn what kind of information is shown.

2. **Read** the graph. Use the labels.

3. **Study** the data. Compare the bars.

4. **Draw conclusions**. Ask yourself questions like the ones on this page.

Skills Practice

1. How many pets are mammals?

2. How many pets are birds?

3. How many more pets are mammals than fish?

Reading a Picture Graph

A second-grade class was asked to choose their favorite season. A picture graph was made to show the results. A picture graph uses pictures to show information.

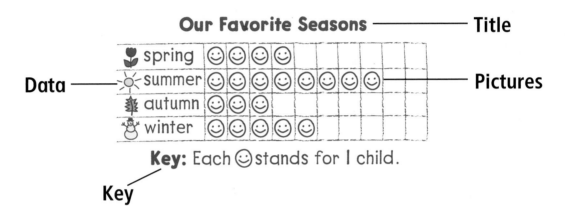

Title — **Our Favorite Seasons**

Data

Pictures

Key: Each ☺ stands for I child.

Key

How to Read a Picture Graph

1. **Look** at the title to learn what kind of information is shown.

2. **Read** the graph. Use the labels.

3. **Study** the data. Compare the number of pictures in each row.

4. **Draw conclusions**. Ask yourself questions like the ones on this page.

Skills Practice

1. Which season did the most classmates choose?

2. Which season did the fewest classmates choose?

3. How many classmates in all chose summer or winter?

Measurements

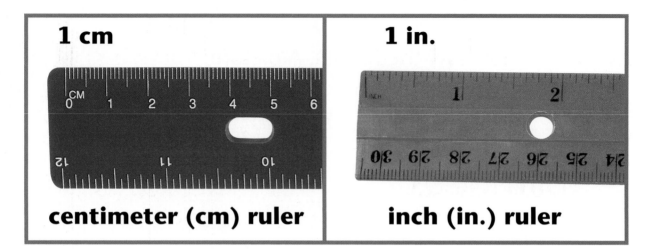

1 cm

centimeter (cm) ruler

1 in.

inch (in.) ruler

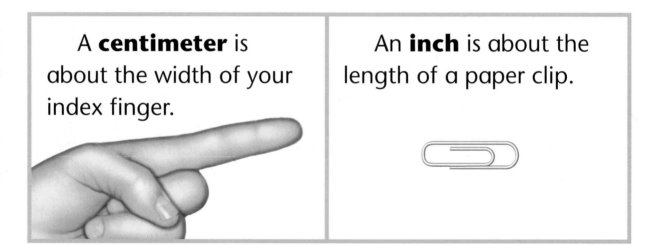

A **centimeter** is about the width of your index finger.

An **inch** is about the length of a paper clip.

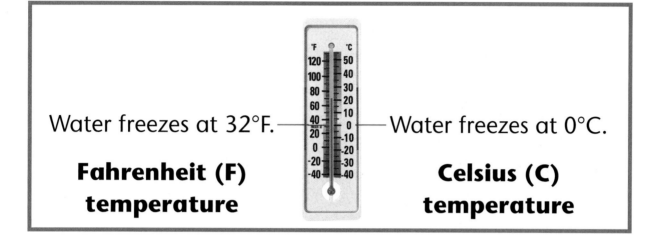

Water freezes at 32°F.

Fahrenheit (F) temperature

Water freezes at 0°C.

Celsius (C) temperature

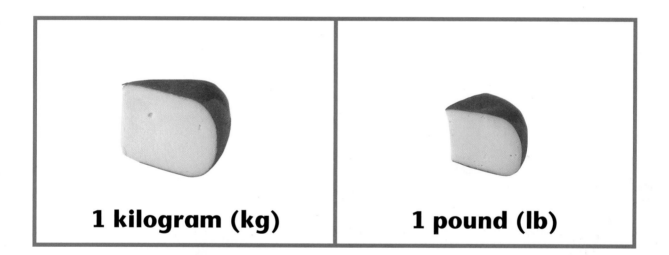

1 kilogram (kg)

1 pound (lb)

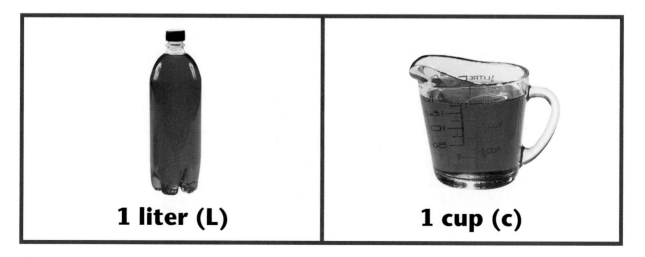

1 liter (L)

1 cup (c)

Safety in Science

Here are some safety rules to follow when you do activities.

1. **Think ahead.** Study the steps and follow them.

2. **Be neat and clean.** Wipe up spills right away.

3. **Watch your eyes.** Wear safety goggles when told to do so.

4. **Be careful with sharp things.**

5. **Do not eat or drink things.**

Glossary

A glossary lists words in alphabetical order. To find a word, look it up by its first letter or letters.

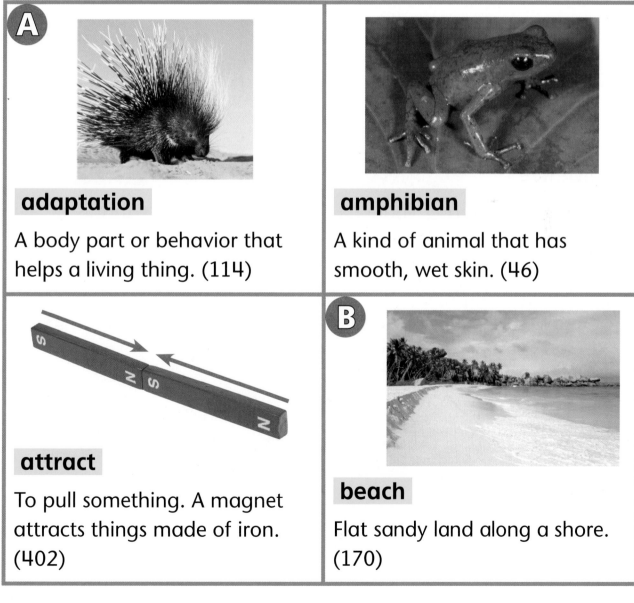

A

adaptation

A body part or behavior that helps a living thing. (114)

amphibian

A kind of animal that has smooth, wet skin. (46)

attract

To pull something. A magnet attracts things made of iron. (402)

B

beach

Flat sandy land along a shore. (170)

bird

The only kind of animal that has feathers. (45)

C

camouflage

A kind of adaptation where an animal's color or pattern helps it hide. (118)

condense

To change from water vapor into tiny water drops. The drops form clouds. (238)

crater

A hole in a surface that is shaped like a bowl. The moon has many craters. (300)

D

desert

Land that gets very little rain. (144)

dissolve

To completely mix a solid with a liquid. (329)

R28

drought

A long time with little rain that causes the land to get very dry. (181)

E

edible

Describes something that is safe to eat. (92)

environment

All the things that are in a place. (108)

erosion

When moving water changes the land by carrying rocks and soil to new places. (182)

evaporate

To change from liquid into water vapor. (238)

F

fall

The season after summer where the air begins to get cooler. (266)

fish

A kind of animal that is covered in scales, uses gills to breathe, and lives in water. (47)

float

To stay on top of a liquid. (330)

flood

When rivers and streams get too full and the water flows onto land. (180)

flowers

The part of a plant that makes fruits. (78)

food chain

A diagram that shows how animals and plants are linked by what they eat. (126)

force

Something that makes an object move or stop moving. (388)

R30

forest

Land that is covered with trees. (138)

fruits

The parts of a plant that hold the seeds. (78)

G

gas

A kind of matter that does not have its own shape. (337)

gills

The part of a fish that takes air from the water. (39)

gravity

A force that pulls things down to the ground. (396)

H

habitat

The place where an animal finds food, water, and shelter. (140)

heat

A kind of energy that makes things hotter. (354)

hill

A high place that is smaller than a mountain and usually round on top. (167)

humus

Pieces of dead plants and animals. Humus, clay, and sand make up soil. (202)

I

inquiry skills

The skills people use to find out information. (12)

insect

A kind of animal that has three body parts and six legs. (48)

L

lake

A body of water with land all around it. (175)

larva

Another name for a caterpillar. (54)

leaves

The parts of a plant that take in light and air to make food. (77)

length

The measure of how long a solid is. (324)

life cycle

All the parts of a plant's or animal's life. (52)

light

A kind of energy that lets us see. (360)

liquid

A kind of matter that flows and takes the shape of its container. (328)

living

Needing food, water, and air to grow and change. (32)

loudness

How loud or soft a sound is. (368)

lungs

The part of some animals that helps them breathe air. Pigs are animals that use lungs to breathe. (39)

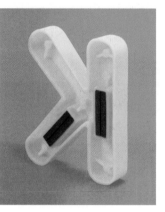

magnet

An object that will attract things made of iron. (402)

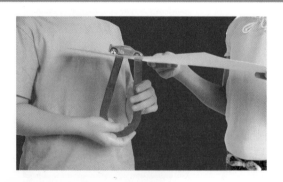

magnetic force

The pulling force of a magnet. (404)

mammal

A kind of animal that has hair or fur and feeds its young milk. (44)

mass

The measure of how much matter something has. You can measure mass with a balance. (324)

matter

Everything around you. Matter can be a solid, liquid, or gas. (314)

migrate

To move to a new place to find food. (268)

mixture

Two or more things that have been mixed together. (322)

moon

A huge ball of rock in the sky that does not give off its own light. (287)

motion

When something is moving. Things are in motion when they move. (382)

mountain

The highest kind of land, with sides that slope toward the top. (166)

natural resource

Anything from nature that people can use. (194)

nonedible

Describes something that is not safe to eat. (93)

nonliving

Not needing food, water, and air and not growing. (33)

nutrients

Minerals in the soil that plants need to grow and stay healthy. (70)

ocean

A large body of salt water. (150, 176)

oxygen

A kind of gas that plants give off and animals need to breathe. People need trees to get oxygen. (123)

P

pitch

How high or low a sound is. (369)

plain

Flat land that spreads out a long way. (168)

pole

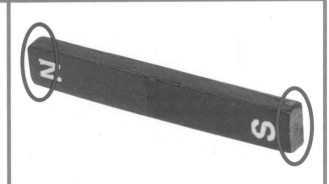

Near an end of a magnet where the pull is strongest. (406)

pollen

A powder that flowers need to make seeds. Bees help carry pollen from one flower to another. (124)

pollution

Waste that causes harm to land, water, or air. (208)

pull

To tug an object closer to you. (389)

pupa

The part of a life cycle where a caterpillar changes into a butterfly. (54)

push

To press an object away from you. (389)

R

recycle

To use old resources to make new things. (211)

reduce

To use less of a natural resource. (210)

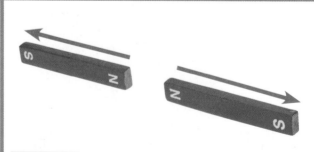

repel

To push away. Poles that are the same on a magnet repel each other. (406)

reptile

A kind of animal that has scaly, dry skin. (46)

reuse

To use a natural resource again. (211)

river

A large body of moving water. (174)

rock

A hard, nonliving thing that comes from Earth. (200)

roots

The part of a plant that holds it in the soil and takes in water and nutrients. (75)

rotate

To spin around like a top. Earth rotates and causes day and night. (292)

S

science tools

The tools that help scientists find what they need. (20)

season

A season is a time of year. The seasons are spring, summer, fall, and winter. (252)

seed coat

A covering that protects a seed. (82)

seeds

The parts of a plant that new plants grow from. (78)

senses

The way we tell what the world is like. The five senses are sight, hearing, smell, taste, and touch. (4)

shadow

A dark place made when an object blocks light. (362)

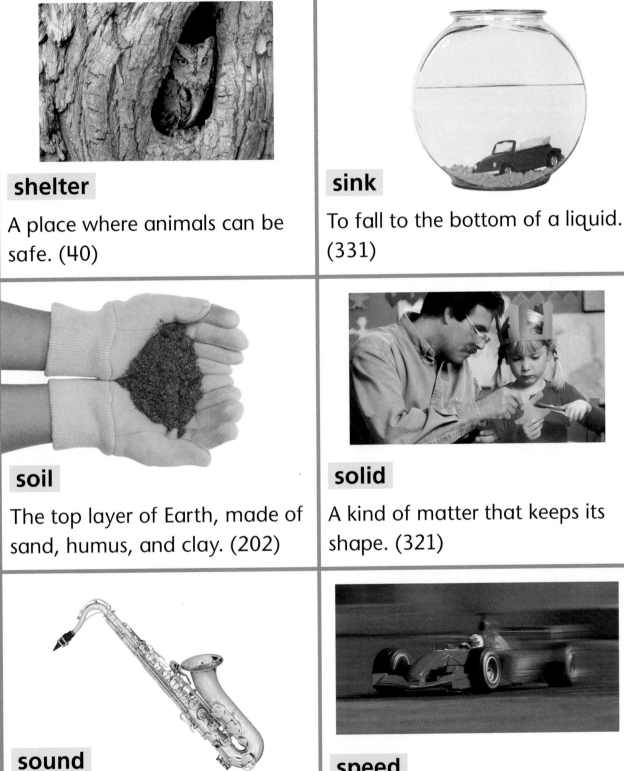

shelter

A place where animals can be safe. (40)

sink

To fall to the bottom of a liquid. (331)

soil

The top layer of Earth, made of sand, humus, and clay. (202)

solid

A kind of matter that keeps its shape. (321)

sound

A kind of energy that you hear. (366)

speed

The measure of how fast something moves. (383)

spring

The season after winter where the weather gets warmer. (254)

star

An object in the sky that gives off its own light. (286)

steam

Gas that comes from boiling water. (340)

stem

The part of a plant that holds up the plant and lets food and water move through the plant. (76)

stream

A small body of moving water that flows downhill. (174)

summer

The season after spring that is usually hot. Summer has many hours of daylight. (260)

sun

The star closest to Earth. (286)

sunlight

Light that comes from the sun. (69)

T

tadpole

A young frog that comes out of an egg and has gills to breathe. (52)

temperature

The measure of how hot or cold something is. You can measure temperature with a thermometer. (232)

thermometer

A tool used to measure temperature. (232)

V

valley

The low land between mountains or hills. (168)

vibrate

To move quickly back and forth. (366)

water cycle

The movement of water from Earth to the air and back again. (238)

water vapor

Water in the air that you can not see. (238)

weather

What the air outside is like. (226)

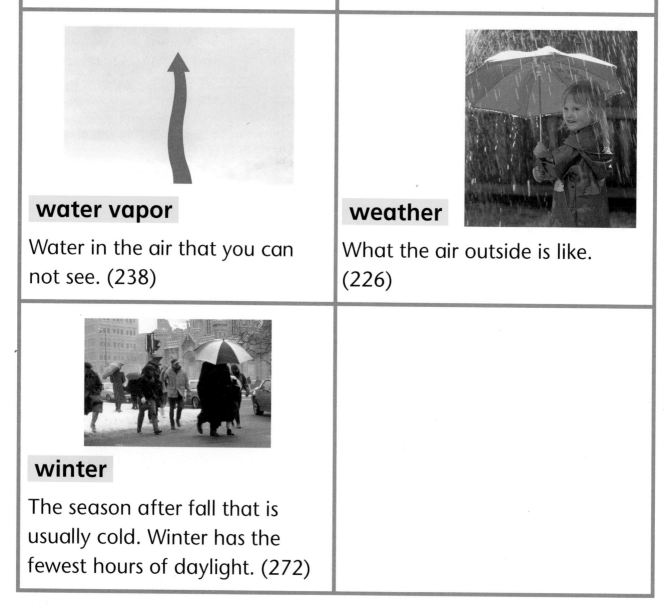

winter

The season after fall that is usually cold. Winter has the fewest hours of daylight. (272)

Index

Photography Credit
Page Placement Key: (t) top; (b) bottom; (c) center; (l) left; (r) right; (bg) background; (fg) foreground; (i) inset.

Cover

(front) Paul Nicklen/National Geographic/Getty Images; (back) Robert & Lorri Franz/Corbis; (back) (bg) Rosemary Calvert/Getty Images;

Front End Sheets

Page 1 (t) Alaska Stock Images; bg) Alaska Stock Images; **Page 2** (t), (b) David W. Hamilton/Getty Images; (bg) Alaska Stock Images; **Page 3** (t) Alaska Stock Images; (b) Joel Sartore/National Geographic/Getty Images; (bg) Alaska Stock Images;

Title Page

Paul Nicklen/National Geographic/Getty Images;

Copyright Page

(inset) Paul Nicklen/National Geographic/Getty Images; (bg) Rosemary Calvert/Getty Images;

Back End Sheets

Page 1 (t) Thomas Mangelsen/Minden Pictures; (b) Norbert Rosing/National Geographic/Getty Images; (bg) Alaska Stock Images; **Page 2** (t) Yva Momatiuk/John Eastcott/Minden Pictures; (c) Paul Nicklen/National Geographic/Getty Images; (b) Alaska Stock Images; (bg) Alaska Stock Images; **Page 3** (t) Klein/Hubert/Peter Arnold, Inc.; (b) Theo Allofs/Visuals Unlimited; (bg) Alaska Stock Images;

Table of Contents: iv Photodisc Green/Getty; vi Alan Majchrowicz; viii Corbis;

Unit A

26 Saint Louis Zoo's Monsanto Insectarium / Todd Davis Photography; 27 AP/Wide World Photos; 28 Randy Wells/Corbis; 32 Getty Images; 34 (tl) Getty Images, (cl) A. & S. Carey/Masterfile, (bl) Paul Zahl/National Geographic Image Collection, (tr) Gary Thomas Sutto/Corbis, (cr) Getty Images, (br) Royalty-Free/Corbis; 35 Getty Images; 36 Michael & Patricia Fogden/Corbis; 38 (t) China Span/Animals Animals/Earth Scenes; (b) Winifred Wisniewski; Frank Lane Picture Agency/ Corbis; 39 Kristian Cabanis/Age Fotostock; 40 (b) D. Robert & Lorri Franz/Corbis, (t) W. Perry Conway/Corbis; 41 D. Robert & Lorri Franz/Corbis; 42 Fritz Poelking/Age Fotostock; 44 (t) David Tipling/Nature Picture Library, (b) Tom Brakefield/Corbis; 45 (t) Robert Lubeck/Animals Animals/ Earth Scenes, (b) John W. Bova/Photo Researchers; 46 (t) Darrell Gulin/Corbis, (c) Santiago Fernandez/Age Fotostock, (t) Marian Bacon/Animals Animals/Earth Scenes; 47 (t) Getty Images, (i) National Geographic/Getty Images, (b) Avi Klapfer/SeaPics.com; 48 (t) Paul Eekhoff/Masterfile, (c) IFA/eStock Photo/PictureQuest, (b) Jim Sugar/Corbis; 49 John W. Bova/Photo Researchers; 50 Norbert Rosing/National Geographic Image Collection; 54 E.R. Degginger/Color-Pic; 57 E.R. Degginger/Color-Pic, (b) Gary Meszaros/Photo Researchers; 61 (bg) PictureQuest; 62 (tl) Robert Lubeck/Animals Animals/Earth Scenes, (tlc) Paul Eekhoff/Masterfile, (trc) Tom Brakefield/Corbis; (tr) Avi Klapfer/SeaPics.com; (b) E.R. Degginger/Color-Pic; 63 John Staples; Cordaly Photo Library Ltd./Corbis; 64 Royalty-free/Corbis; 66 Carolynn Shelby/Alamy Images; 68 Freeman Patterson/ Masterfile; 69 Tom Stewart/Corbis; 75 (l) Visuals Unlimited, (r) Paul Souders/IPNSTOCK.com, (bg) Alamy Images; 76 Gordon R. Gainer/Corbis; 77 (tl) Royalty-free/Corbis, (tr) Charles Mauzy/Corbis, (bl) Rob and Ann Simpson/Visuals Unlimited, (br) Barry Runk/Grant Heilman Photography; 78 (t) Bill Ross/Corbis, (b) Digital Vision (Royalty-free)/Getty Images; 80 Getty Images; 82 (c) Jerome Wexler/Photo Researchers, 83 (l) Michael P. Gadomski/Photo Researchers, (r) Jeff Lepore/Photo Researchers; 84 (c) David Sieren/Visuals Unlimited 85 (t) Ned Therrien/Visuals Unlimited; 86 (tr) Getty Images, (c) D. Cavagnaro/DRK, (tl) Mary Ellen Bartley/PictureArts/Corbis; 87 Ned Therrien/ Visuals Unlimited; (b) Jerome Wexler/Photo Researchers; 88 Digital Vision (Royalty-free)/Getty Images; 90 (bg) Panoramic Images, (t) Valerie Giles/Photo Researchers, 91 (t) Michael Gadomski/ Animals Animals/Earth Scenes, (b) George Harrison/Grant Heilman Photography; 92 Getty Images; 93 Liz Barry/Lonely Planet Images; 95 Bill Ross/Corbis; 99 (bg) Getty Images, Roger Wilmshurst; Frank Lane Picture Agency/Corbis; 101 Ken Wardius/Index Stock Imagery;

Unit B

102 Tom and Pat Leeson; 103 Dr. Norm Lownds, Curator, 4-H Children's Garden; 104 National Geographic/Getty Images; 106 William Ervin/Photo Researchers; 108 Patti Murray/Animals Animals/Earth Scenes; 110 Getty Images; 111 Patti Murray/Animals Animals/Earth Scenes; 112 Kevin Leigh/Index Stock Imagery; 114 (b) Alamy Images, (t) Alamy Images; 115 (t) Niall Benvie/ Corbis, (bl) Francois Gohier/Photo Researchers; 116 (bg) T. Allofs/Zefa, (t) Roland Seitre/Peter Arnold, Inc., (c) Norman Owen Tomalin/Bruce Coleman, Inc.; 117 (l) Alamy Images, (r) ABPL Image Library/Animals Animals/Earth Scenes; 118 (tl) Yva Momatiuk/John Eastcott/Minden Pictures, (tr) Tom Walker/Visuals Unlimited, (bl) Seapics.com, (bc) Ken Thomas/Photo Researchers, (br) Bernard Photo Productions/Animals Animals/Earth Scenes; 120 John Vucci/Peter Arnold, Inc.; 122 (t) Galen Rowell/Corbis, (bl) Alamy Images, (br) Bruce Coleman, Inc.; 123 McDonald Wildlife Photography/Animals Animals/Earth Scenes; 124 (l) Jonathan Blair/National Geographic Image Collection, Wild & Natural/Animals Animals/Earth Scenes; 125 (t) Eric and David Hosking/Corbis, John Pontier/Animals Animals/Earth Scenes; 127 John Vucci/Peter Arnold, Inc.; 131 (bg) Creatas Royalty Free Stock Resources; 134 Brand X Pictures/PictureQuest; 136 Alamy Images; 138 Grant Heilman/Grant Heilman Photography; 139 (t) Sharon Cummings/Dembinsky Photo Associates, (b) Hal Horwitz/Corbis, 140 (t) Photodisc Green (Royalty-free)/Corbis, (i) D. Robert Franz/Bruce Coleman, Inc., (b) Getty Images; 141 Getty Images; 142 Sally A. Morgan; Ecoscene/Corbis; 144 (bg) Andrew Brown; Ecoscene/Corbis, (t) Donald F. Thomas/Bruce Coleman, Inc.; 145 Getty Images; 146 (t) Joe McDonald/Corbis, (lc) Craig K. Lorenz/Photo Researchers, (b) Ted Levin/Animals Animals/Earth Scenes; 147 Andrew Brown; Ecoscene/Corbis; 148 Amos Nachoum/Corbis; 150 (bg) Dana Hursey/Masterfile, (t) Dana Hursey/Masterfile, (b) Zefa/Photex/E. Bradley/Masterfile; 151 (t) Alamy Images, (b) Photodisc Green (Royalty-free)/Getty Images; 153 Dana Hursey/Masterfile; 157 (bg) Stephen Frink/Corbis; 158 (l) Photodisc Green (Royalty-free)/Getty Images, (c) Craig K. Lorenz/Photo Researchers, (r) Getty Images; 159 Robert Yin/Corbis;

Unit C

160 Royalty-Free/CORBIS; 161 Photo courtesy of USDA-Natural Resouces Conservation Service, Pennsylvania; 162 Dave Jacobs/Index Stock Imagery; 164 (c) Leo and Dorothy Keeler/Accent Alaska. com; 166 Lynn & Sharon Gerig/Tom Stack & Associates; 167 Alan Majchrowicz/Getty Images; 168 Gary Yeowell/Getty Images; 169 (fg) William Manning/Corbis; 170 John Garrett/Corbis; 172 W. Cody/Corbis; 174 (t) James randklev/Getty Images; (b) Nathan Benn/Corbis; 175 Yann Arthus-Bertrand/Corbis; 176 Doug Wilson/Corbis; 178 Owaki-Kulla/Corbis;180 Doug Wilson/ Corbis;181 (br) Bruce Davidson/Nature Picture Library; (tr) Bruce Davidson/Nature Picture Library; 182 David Muench/Corbis; 186, (t) AP/Wide World Photos, (b) NASA. 190 Garry Black/Masterfile; 192 Johnathan Smith; Cordaly Photo Library Ltd./Corbis; 194 Getty Images; 195 (l) Jose Luis Pelaez/ Corbis; 196 (t) Getty Images, (l) Workbookstock.com; 197 Getty Images; 198 Getty Images; 200 (t) Gerald and Buff Corsi/Visuals Unlimited, (b) Lee Snider/Photo Images/Corbis; 201 (t) Getty Images, (ti) Breck P. Kent Photography, (b) Photodisc Green(Royalty-free)/Getty Images, (bi) Massimo Listri/Corbis; 203 (t) David Young-Wolff/PhotoEdit, (b) Paul A. Souders/Corbis; 205 Charles O'Rear/Corbis; 206 Play Mart, Inc.; 209 (t) Stockbyte/PictureQuest, (b) Kathy McLaughlin/The Image Works; 211 David Young-Wolff/PhotoEdit; 213 Alamy Images; 217 (bg) National Geographic/ Getty Images; 218 (t) Myrleen Cate/Index Stock Imagery, (cb) Photodisc Green (Royalty-free)/Getty Images (b) Getty Images; 219 Angela Hampton; Ecoscene/Corbis;

Unit D

220 Jonathan Blair/CORBIS; 221 AP/Wide World Photos; 222 Michael Deyoung/Age Fotostock; 224 Getty Images; 226 (bg) Leng/Leng/Corbis. (t) Mark Polott/Index Stock Imagery, (b) William Manning/Corbis; 227 Craig Tuttle/Corbis; 228 (bg) Digital Vision, (b) Royalty-free/Corbis; 229 Mark Polott/Index Stock Imagery; 233 Workbookstock.com; 234 (t) Jeff Greenberg/Index Stock Imagery, (c) Tony Freeman/PhotoEdit; 236 Jim Reed/Corbis; 240 (t) Royalty-free/Corbis, (c) Jonathan Nourok/PhotoEdit, (b) Royalty-Free/Corbis; 241 Royalty-free/Corbis; 245 Bruce Peebles/Corbis; 247 (tl) Tony Freeman/PhotoEdit, (br) Jeff Greenberg/Index Stock Imagery; 248 Stephen Wilkes/Getty Images; 253 Matheisi/Taxi/Getty Images; 254 (b) Bob Thomas/Stone/Getty Images; (t) Richard Hutchings/PhotoEdit; 255 (fg) Eric Cricton/Corbis; (bg) Pat O'Hara/CORBIS; 256 (b) Royalty-Free/CORBIS; (t) ColorPic, Inc.; 257 Bob Thomas/Getty Images; 258 (c) Network Productions/The Image Works; 260 (l) Photomondo/Getty Images; 261 (fg) Christi Carter/ Grand Heilman Photography; (bg) Alamy Images; 262 (t) Digital Vision/Getty Images; (b) Phil Schermeister/CORBIS; 263 Christi Carter/Grant Heilman Photography; 264 David Allen Brandt/ Stone/Getty Images; 266 (t) James Frank/Alamy Images; (b) Journal Courier/The Image Works; 267 (fg) John Colwell/Grant Heilman Photography; (bg) Robert Estall/CORBIS; 268 (b) Chase Swift/ CORBIS; (t) Florian Moellers/Age Fotostock; 270 Murray Lee/Age Fotostock; 272 (t) James Frank/ Alamy Images; (c) Robert Frerck/Odyssey/Chicago; 273 (fg) Eric and David Hosking/CORBIS; (fg) Werner Dieterich/Getty Images; 274 (b) Royalty- Free/CORBIS; (t) Joseph Van Os/The Image Bank/Getty Images; 275 James Frank/Alamy Images; 276, (tr) Susan Findlay/Master file, (cl) B&C Alexander/Photo Researchers Inc., (r) Alan Fortune/Animals Animals, 277, B&C Alexander/Photo Researchers; 278, Courtesy The Lumpkin Family; 279 (bg) W. Cody/Corbis; 282 Astrofoto/Peter Arnold, Inc.; 284 Creative Concept/Index Stock Imagery; 286 Getty Images; 287 Roger Ressmeyer/ Corbis; 288 Stocktrek/Corbis; 289 G. Kalt/Masterfile; 290 Corbis; 292 Getty Images; 293 Zefa Visual Media - Germany/Index Stock Imagery; 296 Corbis; 298 (bg) Rev. Ronald Royer/Science Photo Library/Photo Researchers, Larry Landolfi/Photo Researchers; 299 Eckhard Slawik/Photo Researchers, Larry Landolfi/Photo Researchers; 300 (bg) NASA/Photo Researchers, (l) Bettmann/ Corbis, (r) NASA/Photo Researchers; 301 (c) 1966 Corbis; Original image courtesy of NASA/Corbis; 305 Gabe Palmer/Corbis; 307 Eckhard Slawik/Photo Researchers, Larry Landolfi/Photo Researchers (b) Alamy Images;

Unit E

308 Albuquerque International Balloon Fiesta, 309 Philip Gould/CORBIS; 310 Photodisc Green/ Getty; 318 Alamy Images; (bg) Dave G. Houser/Corbis; 320 Jose Luis Pelaez, Inc./Corbis; 321 Jose Luis Pelaez, Inc./Corbis; 336 (l) Craig Hammell/Corbis, (r) Francisco Cruz/Superstock; 337 Corbis; 338 Getty Images; 339 Getty Images; 345 (bg) Digital Vision(Royalty-free)/Getty Images; 347 Getty Images;

Unit F

348 Louisville Slugger Museum; 349 Duomo/CORBIS; 350 Ariel Skelley/Corbis; 352 "Courtesy NASA/JPL-Caltech"; 354 Doug Stamm/Stammphoto.com; 356 (cl) Royalty-Free Corbis, (bl) Michael Newman/Photo Edit; 357 Royalty-Free Corbis; 362 (t) Workbookstock.com, (b) Gibson Stock Photography; 364 Tom & Dee Ann McCarthy/Corbis; 368 (t) David Young-Wolff/Photo Edit, (b) Scott Barrow, Inc./SuperStock; 369 (br) Eduardo Garcia/Getty Images; 370 (tl) Spencer Grant/Photo Edit, (tr) Photodisc Blue/Getty Images, (bl) Spencer Grant/Photo Edit; 376 (tc) Michael Newman/Photo Edit, (b) Gibson Stock Photography; 377 Tony Freeman/Photo Edit; 378 Bill Bachmann/Photo Edit; 380 Bob Gelberg/Masterfile; 380 (bg) Ron Watts/Corbis, (i) Photodisc/ Getty 383 (t) Peter Walton/Index Stock Imagery; (b) Myrleen Ferguson Cate/Photo Edit; 384 (t) Bill Stevensen/SuperStock, (cl) Spencer Grant/Photo Edit, (cr) Mark E. Gibson/Corbis, (b) Wally McNamee/Corbis; 385 Bill Stevensen/SuperStock; 386 David Woods/Corbis; 390 (bg) Alamy Images; (b) Table Mesa Prod/Index Stock Imagery; 391 Myrleen Ferguson Cate/Photo Edit; 393 Myrleen Ferguson Cate/Photo Edit; 394 Tony Freeman/Photo Edit; 396 Patrik Giardino/Corbis; 397 (b) Gary Kreyer/Grant Heilman Photography, Inc.; 399 Tony Freeman/Photo Edit; 400 David Lassman/ Syracuse Newspapers/The Image Works; 412 (bl) Wally McNamee/Corbis, (br) Spencer Grant/ Photo Edit; 413 (t) Gary Kreyer/Grant Heilman Photography, Inc., (b) Tony Freeman/Photo Edit;

All other photos © Harcourt School Publishers. Harcourt Photos provided by the Harcourt Index, Harcourt IPR, and Harcourt photographers; Weronica Ankarorn, Victoria Bowen, Eric Camden, Doug Dukane, Ken Kinzie, April Riehm, and Steve Williams.

SELF-PROTECTION An arctic fox curls up in the snow. Then it covers its nose and face with its tail.

YOUNG An arctic fox gives birth to 4-11 pups at a time.

BEHAVIOR The arctic fox stores food during the summer.

CAMOUFLAGE The arctic fox has fur that changes color with the season.

SELF-PROTECTION Thick fur keeps an arctic fox's feet warm.